IMAGES OF WAR
Norwich Blitz

IMAGES OF WAR
Norwich Blitz

RARE PHOTOGRAPHS FROM WARTIME ARCHIVES

MARTIN W. BOWMAN

Pen & Sword
MILITARY

First published in Great Britain in 2012 by
PEN & SWORD MILITARY
an imprint of
Pen & Sword Books Ltd,
47 Church Street, Barnsley,
South Yorkshire.
S70 2AS

Copyright © Martin W. Bowman 2012

ISBN 978-1-84884-755-2

A CIP catalogue record for this book is available
from the British Library

Typeset by Mac Style, Beverley, East Yorkshire
Printed and bound in Great Britain by CPI Group (UK) Ltd, Croydon, CR0 4YY

Pen & Sword Books Ltd incorporates the imprints of
Pen & Sword Books Ltd incorporates the Imprints of Pen & Sword Aviation,
Pen & Sword Family History, Pen & Sword Maritime, Pen & Sword Military, Pen & Sword
Discovery, Wharncliffe Local History, Wharncliffe True Crime, Wharncliffe Transport,
Pen & Sword Select, Pen & Sword Military Classics, Leo Cooper, The Praetorian Press,
Remember When, Seaforth Publishing and Frontline Publishing

For a complete list of Pen & Sword titles please contact:
PEN & SWORD BOOKS LIMITED
47 Church Street, Barnsley, South Yorkshire, S70 2AS, England.
E-mail: enquiries@pen-and-sword.co.uk
Website: www.pen-and-sword.co.uk

This book is dedicated to the firemen and firewomen and the other services
E. C. LeGrice FRPS, Clifford Temple, George Swain and the other brave and resourceful
war photographers who risked their lives during the bombing raids on Norwich in
WW2 to photograph the destruction at close quarters.

House on Exeter Street off Dereham Road with letters proclaiming that the family were all safe at Tasburgh. Someone has scrawled the ironic message 'Bed & Breakfast' over the top right hand window.

Acknowledgements

I am especially grateful to Bob Collis who graciously made available his account of the *Baedeker* raids on Norwich and which is referred to throughout. I am also indebted to Norman Bacon, Mike Bailey; Nigel McTeer; Jack Richardson; Norwich 2nd Air Division Memorial Library; Norwich Castle Museum; Sallie Watson; and Tony Hatch.

Norwich City Hall Isn't Paid for Yet but never Mind, the Luftwaffe will soon put paid to it

On Tuesday, 9 July 1940, a warm afternoon, the dull throb of aircraft engines could be heard from high in the sky near Norwich. At Mousehold aerodrome on the outskirts of the city no air-raid siren was sounded. At Barnards Iron Works, a collection of First World War hangars and outbuildings, there was no cause for alarm. Although the Battle of Britain was about to start the cathedral city was not yet in the front line. When an air raid warning was sounded, a young teenager, Derek Patfield, took his place as one of the pairs of spotters in the watch tower erected on the top of the Enquiry Office, watching for enemy attack. To relieve the boredom he often trained his pair of powerful binoculars on the young female employees walking between the workshops and offices. If he saw approaching enemy aircraft, or thought they identified one as enemy Derek pressed the alarm siren, which sounded all over the works resulting in the employees dashing to the air-raid shelters. When the young spotters got fed up with the lack of aircraft activity during their two-hour shift, they would sound the siren, just for the hell of it, to see the panic it caused! False alarms were explained away as 'incorrect identification'.

At five o'clock when the two aircraft approached from the northeast, flying at about 600 feet, they made out the black markings in the shape of crosses on the wings they flung themselves to the ground. They were Dornier Do 17s! Barnard's was hit by twelve 50kg high-explosive bombs. Three bombs, which failed to explode, were also dropped. The raid was all over in six long seconds. Two men who were working by the loading dock were killed and another threw himself to the ground 20 yards from where a bomb exploded but his only injury was a damaged toe, which later had to be amputated. One worker had a most remarkable escape when a bullet or bomb splinter went through his trouser-leg while others pierced the walls on either side of him. One of the aircraft was seen to bank away towards the centre of the city.

At the famous Colmans' Mustard Works at Carrow, workers coming off shift poured through the main gates – jostling, laughing and bicycle-bells ringing. As the Dorniers suddenly appeared overhead many of the women were pushing their bicycles up Carrow Hill. The Dorniers banked a little and dived and the sound of a whistling bomb rent the air. The older men remembering the sound of falling bombs from the First World War threw themselves to the ground, at the same time shouting to the women, 'Down!' The women and girls did not immediately abandon their bicycles and they did not throw themselves to the ground. A bomb crashed through trees at the top of Carrow Hill near the Black Tower and exploded at ground level. The resulting blast and flying splinters of stones, earth and glass killed Bessie Upton (36) and Maud Balaam (40) instantly. Gladys Sampson (18) and Bertha Playford (19) died shortly after being admitted to the Norfolk and Norwich Hospital. Maud Burrell (37) finally succumbed to her injuries on 12 July. A further four bombs hit the Boulton & Paul works in Riverside killing seven men and three men died later of their injuries. Four men were killed when one of four bombs dropped on the LNER locomotive sheds and goods yard at Thorpe Station exploded. Three others died later of their injuries.

On 2 December 1940 a bomb fell in the grounds of Carrow Abbey and another on Bracondale which killed Mr. Arthur John Pennymore (55), a member of the counting house staff at Colman's who was on duty as a special constable.

Norwich, in common with most English cities, suffered enemy attack from the air and, during a period of almost three and a half years bombs were dropped in every part. 'To most young people' recalled J. Fincham 'the year 1940 meant nothing, but to me it was my first taste of the bomb dropping, which was to take place in Norwich in the next three years. I was at Boulton & Paul in the box shop with Charlie Banfield as my foreman. On Thursday, 1 August I was working a bench drill next to a young lad, Alfred Swan, when suddenly the hooter went – one, two, three, seconds: 'Duck Swanny!' I shouted – and under the bench we dived. Perhaps another two seconds then the bomb hit the canteen killing nine workers with injuries to about 20 more. We were about 50 feet away with a wall in between and were covered with anything that happened to be blown our way. Thank God, on picking ourselves up we found we did not have a mark on us. But by this time the place was on fire which resulted in its complete destruction.'

Mrs. L. F. Kellow, who was living in Mill Hill Road particularly, recalls an incendiary raid in 1941: 'Our garden adjoined the gardens of houses in Park Lane. Two of these were hit by a group of incendiary bombs during the night and despite every effort were soon burning furiously. In an upstairs bedroom facing our home hung a large picture of Queen Victoria portrayed in old age. At first we could see her through the window amid the flames' brilliant light – stern, uncompromising, resolute. The roof fell in, the window and all came down. Still she remained on the inner wall surveying the devastation. Finally, after what seemed an age, she fell and was consumed by the flames. I was young then and that picture and situation made a deep impression on me as recording the spirit of those times.'

One of the few ways Britain had of taking the war to the enemy and lifting spirits and flagging morale was RAF Bomber Command. In a famous rallying cry to his 'old lags' Sir Arthur Harris, Chief of RAF Bomber Command said: 'The Germans entered this war under the rather childish delusion that they were going to bomb everybody else and nobody was going to bomb them. At Rotterdam, London, Warsaw and half a hundred other places, they put that rather naive theory into operation. They sowed the wind and now they are going to reap the whirlwind … When this storm bursts over Germany they will look back to the days of Lübeck and Rostock and Cologne as a man caught in the blasts of a hurricane will look back to the gentle zephyrs of last summer. It may take a year, it may take two, but to the *Nazis* the writing is on the wall. Let them look out for themselves. The cure is in their own hands …'

Norwich was one of those half a hundred other places. In the spring and summer of 1942 this famous cathedral city was one of several singled out by Adolf Hitler the *Nazi* leader for *Terrorangriff* (terror attacks) or reprisal raids by *Luftwaffe* bombers after 234 RAF bombers, mostly carrying incendiaries, had obliterated 200 acres of the old Hanseatic City of Lübeck on Palm Sunday, 28/29 March. This had been followed by incendiary raids on Rostock for four consecutive nights beginning on 23/24 April. By the end only 40% of the city was left standing.

'Reprisal raids' and 'terror attacks' were not new. Following the bombing of London by the *Luftwaffe* during the Battle of Britain RAF Bomber Command retaliated with a raid on Berlin. After the centre of Coventry was ripped asunder on the evening of 14 November 1940, 200 RAF bombers set out on 16/17 December to destroy Mannheim. Coventry was an industrialised city with many war factories but the citizens of cities like Norwich, Exeter and Bath seemed to have little to fear except for sporadic raids and a few bombs that fell. Prior to April 1942 Norwich endured 27 raids at a cost of 81 civilian dead. But these sorties had been ill-defined and small-scale and furthermore, the city was not attacked for eight months. People had become blasé about the threat. 'The ... comparative calm,' wrote Ralph Mottram 'had induced a certain number of citizens to disregard the siren and not to seek the shelters'. The local authorities had grown equally lax. So little used were some public shelters that the council had decided to lock them to prevent them being vandalised. Such complacency was to have fatal consequences. When on 14 April 1942 the *Luftwaffe* began a series of attacks on Norwich and the East Coast, flying in below 3,000 feet to avoid radar contact and flying home again at flat out at speeds approaching 300 mph to make the task of interception very difficult, no-one in Eastern England could foresee the destruction that would soon follow.

On 24 April Baron Gustav Braun von Sturm, Deputy of the German Foreign Office Foreign Press Department, said, 'We shall go out and bomb every building in Britain marked with three stars in the *Baedeker Guide* [sic – Karl Baedeker's series of guide books never marked any buildings with more than two stars!]'. Adolf Hitler had ordered a series of terror attacks mainly against English cities of historic or aesthetic importance, but little strategic value in reprisal for RAF Bomber Command raids on German cities.

Exeter was bombed on 23 April and was followed by Bath. Norwich, a city of 126,000 citizens, was the third target in the *Baedeker* series of raids that would kill a total of 1,637 people, injure 1,760 and destroy 50,000 buildings.

Hitler's warped mind was matched by minions like Walter Darre the German Minister of Agriculture who in April 1942 said:

'As soon as we beat England, we shall make an end of you Englishmen once and for all. Able-bodied men and women will be exported as slaves to the Continent. The old and weak will be exterminated. All men remaining in Britain as slaves will be sterilised; a million or two of the young women of the Nordic type will be segregated in a number of stud farms where, with the assistance of picked German sires, during a period of 10 or 12 years, they will produce annually a series of Nordic infants to be brought up in every way as Germans. These infants will form the future population of Britain ... Thus, in a generation or two, the British will disappear.'

* * *

ir senses; they belong to a class of
u have first knocked out their teeth.

Propaganda referring to the
Norwich.

high cloud, 12 mile visibility and bright
identified on radar heading for Norwich
laid mines off the coast. Only three AI
hters, nine Beaufighters and ten Spitfires
rotected by enough anti-aircraft batteries.
the raiders were shot down. The 'Alert'
e 111 pathfinders of 2/KGr.100 dropped
dive to drop their incendiary bombs and
een 23 and 26 Dornier 217s, Heinkels and Ju
plosive bombs and incendiaries over the city
ombs fell near the M&GN (City) Station that
estroyed. The fires that were started became
om 23.40 to 00.45 hours by KG2 *Holzhammer*
530 with Ju 88s and He 111s of IV/KG55 and
een 300 feet and 15,000 feet, several making
light AA gun sites had engaged the enemy, but
opped 185 HE (High Explosive) bombs and
h, killing 162 people and injuring 600 more.
face shelter in Raynham Street near the Dolphin
water pumping station was put out of action,
people were dug out of the rubble alive.

thousands or building

Opposite the Waterworks at No. 91 lived Michael Bailey (8) and his mother Margaret. Her husband, Hubert, was a soldier in the Army, serving King and Country in Iceland. Mike's best friend was Reginald Edward Wright, known as Reggie, eleven years old; bigger, with dark hair that hung down over one eye. His dark and swarthy complexion made him appear almost Spanish. Reggie was an only child who lived with his mother at 11 Little Armes Street. His father, AC1 Reginald William Wright, was away serving in the RAF. That night Mike nipped round to Reggie's for tea. When he left, Mike said, 'See you tomorrow, Reg'. Late that night Mike's mother said 'Mike — come on hurry up, get out of bed, the siren has gone'. The approaching bombers' engines could be heard. Mike quickly put on his dressing gown over his pyjamas. In the back garden he stood rooted to the spot by the sight of white flares descending like a staircase and illuminating the city like day. Mr. and Mrs. Bloom, an elderly couple who lived at No. 93 appeared and said 'Come into our shelter with us. We'll all keep each other company'. Mike and his mother had just got into the Anderson shelter in the Blooms' back garden when BANG! There was an explosion right near. Mike recalls: 'The raid seemed to go on for hours. When it finally ended we had great difficulty getting out of the shelter because the garden was full of bricks and rubble. Our back door of our house was off and was down the garden. Tiles were off the roof, windows were out and inside, our doors were blown open; the front door was laid across the sofa, plaster was off the walls and ceilings, there was white dust everywhere and paper was hanging in strips, but some daffodils in a vase in a corner of the living room on top of the Bush wireless set were untouched!'

The Baileys, who were now 'bombed out', left next day to stay with their Great Aunt and Uncle at Hillcrest Road, Thorpe on the outskirts of the city. They had a spare room because their son, Teddy Dye, was away in the RAF. He was a flight engineer on Lancasters. Michael was beside himself. 'Reggie won't know where I am' he said. Some days later when Margaret Bailey scanned the casualty lists she said, 'You won't see your friend Reggie again. He was killed on Monday night.' Reggie had stayed at his Grandmother and Grandfather's shelter in the back garden of their house at 6 Little Armes Street. Albert Edward Fuller (57) a painter and decorator and his wife Sarah Agnes Fuller (60) and Reggie Wright were killed instantly when the house took a direct hit and their Anderson shelter was blown out of the ground. All the terraced houses on one side of the street had gone. All that could be seen was sky. At Reggie's home his mother survived but her hair turned grey overnight.

Eighteen year old Nora Norgate lived in a terraced house at 31 Belvoir Street with her elder sister and younger brother and an aunt.

'The air-raid sirens began their mournful wailing at about 11pm. We stirred in our beds waiting for the distinctive sound of the hooter, which told us enemy bombers were getting closer. It went almost immediately as we scrambled from our beds, hurriedly dressed, grabbed our torches and had just began to race downstairs and out to the Anderson shelter in our backyard when the first of many bombs came whistling down. We cowered helplessly on the stairwell in the middle of our house hearing the frightening whine of falling bombs, the awful droning of the enemy planes and the house-shaking explosions. Then the windows suddenly shattered and were blown inwards, closed doors were blasted open, ceilings cracked, then collapsed in clouds of choking dust around us. We were absolutely terrified and were convinced we wouldn't live to see the morning. My sister, aunt and I clung closely together while wondering if my younger brother, who was at that time a messenger for the Air Training Corps, was in the immediate area. It later transpired that he was quite safe. Flares lit up the whole city like daylight as they floated down from the stream of bombers, dozens of swaying searchlight beams, streams of bright tracer bullets were flying, anti-aircraft guns booming defiance. I can't remember how long it all lasted, but it seemed forever.

'When we could no longer hear the bombers overhead we ventured out into the street. Shocked, shaken and in tears, we saw an unbelievable scene of destruction. Most of the houses in Belvoir Street were damaged. A few had been reduced to scattered piles of fiercely burning matchwood and rubble. Many people had been killed, even more injured, some seriously. Other areas of the city had been hit much harder. By some miracle Number 31 appeared to have been one of the least damaged houses in the street, but it would be some time before we got our windows replaced and all the repairs completed.

'The sound of the anti-aircraft gunfire, the strict 'black-out,' the Air Raid Precaution warden, the food and clothing ration books issued to each family, gas-mask drills, steel helmets at work, sleepless nights in the shelters, shortages and long queues for everything, and evacuation drills, became a part of every-day life. Many people were so apprehensive that they left the city during the nights, sleeping in any kind of shelter available in the surrounding countryside and returned to their homes the following morning. During the next seven or eight days after those two air raids, our family would leave our home after tea, walk out of the city, carrying blankets, pillows, sandwiches, hot tea in flasks and our torches to the Mile Cross Bridge and sleep under the bridge each night. We were up early the following morning, walked home and then went to our various places of work.'

Ted Harvey, an NFS section leader who later became Assistant Divisional Officer with the Norfolk Fire Service, recalled:

'Parachute flares lit up the city and almost immediately this was followed by the series of explosions as each 'stick' of bombs took effect. Mixed with the high explosive bombs were the incendiaries and in no time at all the glow of large fires became visible all over the city. The divisional fire control at Bethel Street was immediately flooded with calls from police, wardens and citizens of the city, nearly 200 calls being received within minutes of the initial attack. The control staff – firemen and firewomen – went into action. Their hours of training had now become a reality. They ordered pumps and appliances from the sub-stations and soon these were racing through the streets of Norwich. But fire calls were being received in stations as fast as telephone lines could carry them and more fires were burning than there were pumps and crews in the city. Reinforcements were ordered by the divisional mobilising officer and appliances began to arrive from all quarters of the region and eventually from as far away as the City of London itself. The local crews worked like demons, pumping from water mains where these were intact. Where they were not, they got to work from steel and canvas dams from flooded bomb craters and from the river through miles of canvas hoses. So busy were the firemen many failed to hear the sirens sounding the 'All Clear'. They worked all through the long night and well into the next day until relief crews from long distances took over.'

Pippa Miller was teaching art and craft at the Blyth School on St. Clement's Hill.

'Our school got a direct hit. This completely destroyed the gymnasium, a building that stood on its own, and also shattered part of the roof of the cookery room. All the glass in the northern end of the building was blown out and even the door locks away at the other end of the school were damaged by the blast. The staff had for some time taken turns in pairs to patrol the grounds at night on fire watching duty. It was the quick thinking of Mr. Hufton, the caretaker, which saved two lives one night. He was a veteran of the First World War and knew all the signs when a raid was on. He shouted orders just in time to the staff on duty to, 'Get Down!'

'After the bomb which hit the school had done its worst, the staff assembled the following morning. It was sunny, but with a biting wind which did not help as we tried to clear up all the debris, the dust and splintered glass. Sharp slivers had even got into the girls' desks and the contents of each one had to be removed to be searched. Everyone got tired of the almost permanent crunching noise of broken glass that was being swept up. It seemed to go on for hours – after which we rested, flat out, beside the Central Hall, revelling in the sun and sheltered from the wind. The Head Mistress would anxiously count her staff and girls each time after raids. Thankfully, we had only one casualty in the whole war directly affecting the school [Brenda Waters, aged 17 who died along with her mother, 15-year old brother and 19-year old sister when their house at 76 Helena Road was hit on 30 April 1942]. Admittedly, there was one morning after many disturbed nights when a member of staff did not appear. But a search revealed that she had only overslept!

'... Officially, I was also a part-time ambulance driver during the war, based at 4 Surrey Street Depot. There I received instruction and carried out various duties. I am thankful to say, though, that the official crews adequately dealt with most troubles. Only once did I have to do my bit – which turned out to be an abortive attempt. My assignment was to drive to the City Hall in pitch darkness. However my way was completely blocked by dozens of hosepipes and gaping holes and I had to give up. Eventually I tried to find my back to the depot in the blackness and was mightily glad of the assistance of a gentleman – whose face I never saw – who offered to guide me back. No headlights were allowed on vehicles then and the glimmer of light we had was no good for finding your way in places you did not know!

'In one raid when fire bombs showered down, I went up on to the roof of the depot with the business end of a hosepipe. Down below a stalwart fellow manned the stirrup pump at full speed and we managed to put out several of the flaming bombs. It was only afterwards that I discovered that the water on the roof where I was standing had become electrocuted. How very wise it had been to wear rubber boots. On another occasion, I had just received my full-length uniform overcoat. Suddenly the 'crash' warning wailed and everyone threw himself or herself flat on the ground where they stood. As I had only just put on my new coat, I stayed upright. It became our normal practice in the flat almost every night when the siren wailed to hastily put on something warm and rush downstairs – complete with the cat – and sleep on a neighbour's hearthrug until we heard the 'All Clear' – the continuous note of the siren. The cat, which was black and white, was named 'P.B.' (Partial Blackout) and once while he was asleep in the sunshine on our tiny balcony, he rolled off. He fell three floors but still survived. Later, we had an Anderson shelter in the garden. But we became almost accustomed to hearing the drone of the enemy aircraft engines at night and watch as flares ringed the city. We felt the crunch of high explosives and the shattering 'crumps' of bombs night after night. Then came the 'All Clear' and with it a blessed opportunity for sleep. The time was always too short with school tomorrow – or rather that morning.'

The RAF's Air Warfare Analysis Section would later conclude that the total weight of High Explosive (HE) in this first raid that hit the Norwich Civil Defence region was 45 tonnes of bombs, 96% of the total dropped. The bombers had dropped 35 x 50 kg; 35 x 250 kg; 52 x 500 kg; 30 x 1000 kg and 2 x 1800 kg HE bombs. There were also 34 bombs of 'unspecified' size and a conservative estimate of 'several hundred' incendiary bombs. No parachute mines were reported. The areas worst hit included the City Station, Angel Road, Elizabeth Fry Road, Southwell Road, Rosebery Road and Dereham Road. During the early part of the raid, water mains were seriously damaged, leading to a water shortage at fire sites in the City both in this and the subsequent attack.

Initial casualty figures of 53 killed were later corrected to 162 killed and 600 injured, making this the worst loss of life in a raid on an East Anglian target in WW2. The area around City

Station, Oak Street and Dereham Road was particularly badly hit. City Police estimated that 7,000 houses were damaged. The Ministry of Home Security reported that Extensive damage was caused, 'mainly to the poorer residential quarter' and that 'considerable damage was done to Public Utilities'.

Two 500kg HE bombs fell on Chapel Field Gardens (fortunately one was unexploded) causing many casualties 'Ossy' Osbiston, a member of the rescue service and later an assessor for the War Damage Commission, recalled:

'At 11.15 enemy aircraft flew on over the coast and the first plane dropped chandeliers over the centre of the city and then at short intervals explosives were dropped at random. The first high explosives fell, one on St. Augustine's School and two on Beer's Bacon factory in Oak Street. I reported to Surrey Street and had to ask for volunteers to come with me to the worst incident at Chapel Field Gardens. I had with me two very good chaps – G. Bevis, a real worker and Bert Jenkins, an excellent First Aid man – and about a dozen skilled labourers. The site was a bad one. Young and old were entombed in an underground shelter. Two sisters, about 15 or 16 [Doris May King (16) and Honor Lilian King (14) both heelers in the shoe trade, who lived at 62 Chapel Field Road], were dead. An elderly man was in a sitting position with smashed legs. I was held by the legs upside down and after injecting morphine into his limbs I managed to saw through his seat and release him and he was passed up to the men above. The next thing was to get out twin children who were also trapped. Their mother was a big woman; I should think around 14 to 15 stone. We were told to keep our heads down because of the unexploded bombs, but about 7am the bomb disposal officer said we could carry on as the bomb was rendered 'harmless' …

'It was thought that we had cleared all live casualties, so we had to report to the depot. The town clerk, Mr. Bernard Storey and city engineer, Mr. H. C. Rowley, asked me to give a report to them for the registration office at Cambridge. I said 'No' and that I wanted to go back with my men and make a final search. They agreed and we returned. We all took up positions in the crater and laid our ears to the ground. Immediately one chap said 'Ossy' I can hear moaning.' I lay down beside him and heard it too. I said: 'Do not use any heavy tools only the hands.' We soon came across a very beautiful young girl dead. She was suffocated, but she was lying on top of an old lady and this had saved her life. Part of a concrete reinforcement had gone through her hand. I cut the iron off and my First Aid man covered it and she was sent to hospital. She recovered, as did the chap with smashed legs. I have heard it said many times that the dug-out had so many dead bodies that they could not be recovered and it was filled in. But this was completely untrue.'

Luftwaffe records indicate that all the bombers involved in the first Norwich raid returned safely.

A Letter from Norwich

Kathleen Pye was a 20-year old Red Cross volunteer and bank worker at the National Provincial in St. Benedict's who lived in Brian Avenue and she wrote a letter just days after the second of the *Baedeker* raids to her brother Charlie, who was serving in the Royal Navy. In it she graphically describes the awful experience of so many ordinary people caught up in the war.

The siren went Monday night about quarter to twelve and about ten minutes later while we were still in bed there was a terrific 'crump'. We got up and came downstairs, grabbing our clothes as we came, and John and I and the dog got under the table and Mum and Dad got under the stairs. There we stayed for a whole hour while the planes roared around and dropped bombs unceasingly. Our doors and windows rattled and we thought we must have had a bomb in our garden.

However, at the end of the raid when we went outside, the house was OK but there was a terrific fire in the city. This was, as we found next day, Wincarnis, Victoria Station and City Station and one or two other fires which started in small houses. Dereham Road was badly bombed and all the Heigham Street area. Beers was burned down and they have since got temporary premises at Harry Pointer's. We only had three panes of glass broken in the bank, but Beryl Gedge is awfully worried as there is nothing left of Wincarnis. The Odol works weren't much damaged on Monday, but in Wednesday night's Blitz they too were gutted and all of the staff except about a dozen of the office staff have been dismissed. They are staying on in an office in the Close but when everything is settled they don't know what will happen to them.

You know Pauline Newby who was in the Pantomime. They lived in Patteson Road and Monday night their house received a direct hit. Mr Newby had put an incendiary out on his chicken shed and came indoors to take his wife and two children down to the shelter. While they were still indoors the house was hit. Pauline was rescued fairly quickly from under the rubble and she could speak to her father who was also buried but neither of them could do anything for themselves.

A fire started and Mr Newby could see the flames creeping up on all sides, but fortunately they were extinguished before he was burned. He was got out at five in the afternoon, having been buried since 1 am and he was conscious all the time. Pauline is now out of hospital but she hurt her back and legs and was suffering from shock. Her Dad had two cuts on his head and bruises and his stomach hurt through the weight of the bricks. About two days later Mrs Newby and Barbara, who was five [Her memorial plaque gives her age as 8; her mother Hilda was 45] were dug out and they were very badly charred. I don't know when they are going to be buried but some people were buried today in a communal grave. Maggie Pratt was bombed out of Elizabeth Fry Road and her furniture is nearly all ruined and the house is uninhabitable. Five Irishmen were killed in her road. This first night we only had about one gun firing and no fighters up and the wretched planes were diving wholesale. That was the worst part of it, they usually began diving over Lakenham and then dropped their loads – we escaped the bombs but it was dreadfully nerve-racking and also the wretched bombs were whistling past and every time this happened we kept ducking down lower. The remainder of Rupert Street was knocked about and (the bombs) absolutely knocked Jimmy Middleton's shop and others in that row off the face of the earth. I can't tell you everywhere that was hit, as it was so widespread. Practically every area had some bombs.

Tuesday night we had another raid, but it was only about a couple of planes and we had some AA fire and no bombs were dropped.

Wednesday night we had yet another and although it only lasted three-quarters of an hour it was worse than anything. Old soldiers of the last war and even people who were in the London Blitz said they never experienced anything like it. It was hell let loose.

To accompany the dive-bombing we had the noise of a lot of AA guns. We were quite pleased to hear that though.

It was awful under the table as we had seen the shambles of houses after the last raid and wondered how we would get on if we were hit. However, when then was a lull we thought we'd be better off in the open, so we got the car rug and coats and tore off down Hall Road, past the Tuckswood and got in a field under a hedge. There were lots of other people there and in other places along the Road, as they seemed to appear from nowhere when the 'All Clear' went. It would have been a marvellous sight had it not been for the destruction. It appeared as though the whole of the city was ablaze and one or two smaller fins on the outskirts. Caleys was burned out in the old building and the wall of one part is all leaning in. The new part near Chapel Field was partly burned and all the windows were broken. Buntings was partially burnt and is not useable. Woolworth's, Curls and Brigg Street and Greens, Red Lion Street and Boots and Saxone are completely gone. It's like a wilderness – just masses of rubble and twisted girders. The Norwich Training College was burned-out but all the girls were safe, although some of them had a narrow escape. The Unthank College was bombed out and Duff Morgan's opposite the church is flattened and burnt. It had a direct hit.

The Carlton had a bomb hole in the side and people were standing about for a whole day looking at it when someone spotted the darned thing. It hadn't gone off. They got it out – it was a dud.

Freeman's house and others in Rowington Road had a direct hit, also Warrington's and another in that row and the blast made the houses opposite uninhabitable. Marshall's was bombed out; the bar part of the Smoke Room and the sitting room lay in Grove Road – a mass of bricks and mortar: Three soldiers in the house next door were trapped in the cellar but were got out and only one was hurt. An old lady died in Warrington's Morrison Shelter, but his wife and daughter were safe, but of course they had to be dug out. Warrington was on duty as a warden and of course he knew exactly where to find them and they were soon rescued.

A land mine dropped at the bottom of Grapes Hill and there's a terrific crater, which extends right across the crossroads. The bank and Hick's fish shop, the ironmongers and Boots etc, are now just a pile of rubble. I think this is one of the worst areas, as another dropped behind the bank and all round there's nothing but piles of bricks and mortar: The only thing standing is the bank's strong room, which was built of reinforced concrete. It has a crack in it through which the fireman managed to squirt some water; but everything inside was safe, although some things are a bit damp. My typewriter, which was on the shelf, fell off and is slightly broken but I think is repairable. Our caretakers were sheltering in the Crown Inn and although the upstairs floors were badly damaged they were safe in the cellar; but they've lost everything and poor Mrs Hare was worried to distraction as her mother had to have both legs off above the knee as a result of Monday's raid. We are operating at London Street at the moment but we don't know what's going to happen to us. We may be merged with Norwich or we may have our own department in one of the side rooms up there. We haven't got everything out yet but what we have is full of small stones and mortar; and of course we've lost quite a lot of stuff in the main office including one or two personal belongings. Although there's such destruction no one was hurt down there, as they were all in shelters further up the road.

Dereham Road got another packet and Beers had more incendiaries up at Harry Pointer's, but it wasn't much. Nearly all the laundries with the exception of the Pearl were bombed and burned and we've lost our laundry, as has half the population of Norwich. The Bowthorpe Institution had a direct hit on the old men's ward and killed one or two, but they were evacuated before Wednesday's raid to make room for the wounded. Then were also some fires on the cemetery and the Angel Road area was bombed. Sheila was bombed out of Hillcrest Road. Arthur Pye was also bombed out of Livingstone Street.

I can't remember any more places in detail now, but you'll see it all when you come home although you won't see it at its worst as they are clearing up already. A shelter in Chapel Field Gardens had a direct hit and many were killed – when they decided the remaining people were dead they sealed it up.

I don't think we'll have any more dive-bombing as Norwich is waking up at last. Eileen Marshall is sleeping here in your bed and Mrs M and Cyril are out at Surlingham and old Billy went to Thetford, but is back again today and is living with Aggie. I went to the Woodlands (Bowthorpe Inst) to help and, my crumbs, did we get some nice jobs. I won't put them on paper. I've also done a duty at Rosebery Road rest centre but it was not quite so bad as the Institution.

Poor old Billy Marshall has no clothes. All his things sailed down into the bar and then on into the cellar with the drawing room furniture on top of it. Cyril's bedroom was cut in two and it was all open to the sky but they couldn't get up there for a couple of days as the rest of the house looks as though it would fall in a high wind. However they've been salvaging today and when he looked in his chest of drawers he found that his new stopwatch and cigarette case were missing. Evidently someone had got up there and pinched them. Some money was also pinched from Freeman's house – or what remains of it. I think there must be some awful people about. Of course all this has its lighter moments and we've had some laughs and we all came through safe – thank God, and I hope we don't have any more.

Well, I must finish now I think this is the longest letter I've ever written and it's taken three sittings to finish it as I've been so busy with Red X – we wanted plenty of blood last weekend. Directly my three months is up they're going to extract another pint from me. That will be sometime after May 15. They want a lot of Group 4 blood, as this is most useful … Well, cheerio and all the best,

Write soon,
Lots of love
From Kathleen. XXXXXX

On the night of 28/29 April an anticipated follow-up raid on Norwich did not materialise – this time. Instead the enemy struck at York, where 50 tonnes of bombs caused destruction and serious fires, 83 people being killed and 92 badly injured, this time, Beaufighters of 68 Squadron at Coltishall were able to make contact with the enemy over the North Sea. Two bombers were claimed shot down; one of which (a He 111) was chased for 50 miles and brought down off Holland. The total enemy losses were five aircraft. The next day (29 April) the British press mentioned the *Baedeker* connection for the first time, the *Daily Mail* carrying an item on the first Norwich raid. 'These 'spite' raids appear to be taxing the *Luftwaffe*'s resources' ran the report. AA Command could not possibly hope to effectively defend all the historic towns and cities in Britain – there simply were not enough guns. However, during 28 April, Mobile Heavy AA units (3.7 inch) and UP (Unrotating Projectiles) 'Z' rocket batteries were hurriedly positioned near Norwich and Ipswich in anticipation of further attacks.

Wednesday 29/30 April 1942

An estimated 75 enemy aircraft operated over Britain and 40 of these carried out a second devastating raid on Norwich in which the bombing was more concentrated on the city's commercial centre. The 'Alert' sounded once more at 11.10pm but the first bombs actually fell at 11.25pm. Several fires were still smoking from the Monday raid, but none were thought to be visible. The weather was again excellent, with no cloud and moonlight. Despite spirited defence from guns and rockets the *Luftwaffe* again used flares and incendiary bombs to good effect. This attack was led by seven He 111 Pathfinders from Chartres. The main bomber force that followed comprised 17 Do 217s of II/KG2 at Soesterberg and eleven of III/KG2 at Schiphol. A further eight Do 217s of I and IV operated from Gilze Rijen. Nine crews came from IV/KG55 and nine from II/KG40 at Soesterberg; five of IV/KG4 and fifteen Ju 88s of IV *Gruppen* of KG3, KG30 and KG77 all from Chievres. The raid lasted about an hour and a quarter during which 112 HE bombs were dropped along with thousands of incendiaries. About half of the 90 tonnes of bombs that were dropped hit the city. The target was the city centre with Thorpe Station and Goods Yard, Bishop Bridge Gas Works, the water tower and the Boulton & Paul works as the secondary targets. Far more incendiaries were used and caused severe damage, made more severe because the water works had been disabled in the previous raid causing major problems for the fire service. Sixty-nine people lost their lives and 89 were injured.

The City Hall remained remarkably undamaged, the nearest bomb landing on the Clover Leaf Cafe on the corner of Lower Goat Lane and St. Giles Street. George Swain, who was prevented from joining up because of a duodenal ulcer, was in his photographic studio at St. Giles, which he ran with his sister Muriel, loading his camera when the world famous Hippodrome next door took a direct hit. Esmond Wilding was taking over the management of the theatre that week. He and Harold Pitchford the retiring manager were standing on the stage-door steps when the bombs fell. The stage manager and the Danish owners of a troupe of performing sea lions were in the indoor shelter of the building near the stage door. Harold Pitchford (44), his wife Gertrude (27) and Dagmar Pederson (53) the sea lions' trainer and her husband Anders Haagen Pederson (56) were killed and the blast blew the two house managers down the steps without injuring them, ripped the back out of the Swain's studio and lifted the stage of the theatre into the air. The stage supports fell but the stage remained four inches above its normal level. From inside of the theatre came a terrible sound – 'a wailing worse than the whistle of a bomb' recalled George Swain. 'It was from one of the sea lions which the bomb had released.' He would never forget the noise it made, flapping its ungainly way through the dark, empty theatre, crying for its master. George, who served as an ARP warden and was a member of the Observer Corps, cycled the city streets at night during the bombing and recorded many unforgettable and unique photos.

Jim Hanly, a special constable, adds: 'S/Inspector Gerald Sturgess and two or three of us were searching in the dark on stage for casualties when there was a series of roaring barks and a great flapping. As we fell into the orchestra pit somebody produced a light and we saw the sealion trying to do a solo act. One wag asked 'anybody got a rubber ball and some lumps of sugar?' Buddy – billed as the World's Greatest Comedy Seal died soon afterwards. Jim Hanly concluded a macabre end to the Hippodrome story. 'A telephone message from London to the police said that one of the fatal casualties was a woman in the cast who was thought to have a considerable sum of money sewn in her corsets. This turned out to be true and the money was recovered before her bloodstained clothing was burnt.'

Certainly this attack hit the City Centre, but the 'spill' of bombs crept E and NE. 'Blitzed' areas included Crooks Place, Orford Place, St. Giles, Duke Street, Newmarket Road and Chapel Field, to mention but a few. This was a far more concentrated attack, which had more effect on commercial buildings and residential property than the first. Fires, fanned by a stiff wind, raged out of control, laying waste to department stores in Brigg Street, St. Stephens and Rampant Horse Street where the scene of dreadful devastation included Curl's and Bunting's department stores and Peacock's Stores. The ancient thatched Boar's Head pub on the corner of Surrey Street and St. Stephen's Street and Caley's chocolate factory were also destroyed. Many children risked life and limb over the ensuing days to get amongst the rubble and into the lower stories of the building where the vats of chocolate had ended up releasing their precious contents. Despite being riddled with dust and masonry children grabbed the chunk of chocolate which had been rationed and gorged themselves; many of them eating so much that they were sick. The area of the city from St. Benedict's Street and along Dereham Road was badly hit on both raids. The area around and including the historic St. Benedict's Gates was reduced to rubble, as were the nearby Wincarnis and Odol works off Westwick Street and large sections of Grape's Hill and Barn Road. St. Benedict's church was reduced to little more than the remnants of a wall and its tower.

Sheila Galey, who had married early that year and whose husband was away in the RAF, had spent Monday night sheltering under the stairs of their house in Hill House Road not far from Thorpe Station as the bombs dropped quite near. On this second raid she went into the shelter in the garden. One bomb fell in the back garden of No. 4 opposite, demolishing it and killing 79-year old widow Mrs. Catherine Eve Edrich. The blast took the front of the Galey's house out completely but left the back wall, kitchen and scullery standing. The next bomb fell in Ella Road so she was exactly mid-way between the two – a split second away from death.

In Ella Road, when the siren sounded five year old Trevor Middleton's mother Gertrude quickly got him out of bed and carried him across the road. Alongside the school wall was a passage which ran between Ella Road and Marion Road. Two air raid shelters had been built but for some reason Trevor's mother took him into the shelter further away from their house. She also called to those in the first shelter to join them. It saved their lives because when a bomb dropped in Ella Road it not only demolished several houses, including the Middleton's but also that first shelter. The next-door neighbour had refused to join them and when their house collapsed they were buried in the debris. Mr. Middleton was working at Laurence Scott's and was an ARP warden. He was quickly on the scene and he managed to dig his way in and pull her out but she had suffocated. [Winifred May Gamble, a 36-year old housewife at 58 Ella Road and Helen Wright, a 78-year old housewife at 1 Ella Road were killed]. Mrs. Middleton carried her son 'piggy-back' fashion up Quebec Road to the makeshift centre at the top of the hill. Trevor looked down from the top of the hill to see Norwich 'all ablaze'. He did not know until 32 years later that this was the night that Norwich received its heaviest raid of the war. Next day Sheila Galey salvaged what she could from the ruins including her wedding presents. A neighbour whose house had escaped damage took a bone china tea set to look after until the war was over.

Edward LeGrice, The author of *Norwich, The Ordeal of 1942* recalled:

'My work as a spare time Photographer for the National Building Record made it necessary for me to photograph such churches and historical buildings as suffered damage through enemy action. The outstanding remembrance is of the choking dust and smell of soot and gas, for the blast certainly acted as a chimney sweeper par excellence. On the night of 29 April our family sheltered under the stairs – I had been told by an expert that a cupboard under a strong staircase offered the best possible protection – and so it proved in our case and in many others. One of the photographs shows the great damage done to a house which had a direct hit, but which left the staircase intact [115]. Bomb after bomb fell shaking the house to its foundations, for we counted 29 HE bombs within a few hundred yards of us. Windows were shattered, ceilings crashed down, the crockery on the cupboard shelves was shaken off, a sugar basin emptied itself on my daughter's head, to be followed by the milk jug, and finally when one bomb fell just opposite, the voice of a warden was heard to say, 'Don't you think you had better come out of there?' We thought we had better come out and happily that proved to be the last one in the district that night. One bomb fell in my garden, and although it hit and smashed the thick branch of an apple tree, took the whole end off my garden hut and made a crater 3 feet across, it failed to explode fortunately for the adjoining houses. This bomb caused the loss of 2,000 precious scientific negatives but I was profoundly thankful that hardly one dozen of my Cathedral negatives were destroyed. The effect of the heat and blast from the falling bomb was very curious. Whole boxes of glass negatives were reduced to fine powder. Each negative was in an envelope, and when opened carefully looked almost undamaged, until it was lifted, when it fell into powder.

'Every wood locker was also shattered to bits and the sides of the hut were drawn apart as much as six inches. For a long time we were unaware the Bomb was there, and lightly walked over the depression which hid it. It was not until sundry misgivings led me to call in the bomb disposal officer that it became certain a 500lb bomb had been just under our feet. Eventually it was dug out, leaving a hole 30 feet deep and six or eight across, to be refilled with the many tons of sand which had been dug out.'

Altogether, 179 fires were attended by NFS crews. Ted Harvey was called out to the Davey Place area:

'Slightly fewer HE bombs fell on the Wednesday night but far more incendiaries were showered on the city. There was a conflagration all around us. We weren't controlling anything. It was just a case of pouring water onto the flames, and in time the sheer amount of water reduced it. But by then the centre was devastated. Buildings had collapsed, particularly those of steel-girdered construction. Timber-framed buildings, funnily enough, stood up to it better. In the end, it was a question of taking a stand and just trying to stop the fires spreading any further.'

An initial casualty figure of 30 killed was eventually corrected to 69, with a further 89 people injured. It was an experience that nobody who lived through it would ever forget. The raiders flew at heights above 500 feet and machine gunning was again reported. A higher proportion of incendiary bombs were used in this raid, but many fell amongst the debris of buildings destroyed two nights earlier and those fires which did break out were mostly separated. A further heavy load of HE bombs however, 39 tonnes, or 92% of the total dropped, fell in the

Norwich area. These comprised 5 x 50 kg; 40 x 250 kg; 23 x 500 kg; 6 x 1000 and 29 HE bombs of 'unspecified' size. No reliable figure was given regarding numbers of incendiary bombs used, for as Air Warfare Analysis Section added in a sad footnote: 'The fireguard appeared to have joined the trekkers (people leaving the area for the open country) on the second night'. The toll would almost certainly have been greater but for a mass exodus which took place between the two raids. Many families had trekked to shelters on the outskirts of the city and some had simply spent the nights in open countryside. An official report claimed that as many as 40,000, a third of the city's population, had taken part in the voluntary evacuation. 'Whole streets and roads were deserted at nightfall for days and weeks afterwards. It was like living in a ghost town,' declared one who chose to stay. It was not so much a case of mass hysteria, as simple common sense.

'There was a quiet spirit of acceptance,' one woman recorded 'and as they tramped out of the city in their hundreds in the evening, a few belongings in an old pram, tired dirty children, a setting sun … suddenly one picture people all over the world doing the same out of Lashio, out of Mandalay, out of Rostock. Everywhere. And in much worse circumstances than dry, springtime Norwich …' The mass trekking only lasted about a week, which was just as well since a number of Civil Defence workers had left too. In one incident, a whole team of fire-watchers abandoned their post. The ravaged city became a breeding ground for wild rumours. There was talk of typhoid outbreaks, of panics and of widespread looting. Few of the stories proved accurate. 'People were frightened, but not cowardly,' one woman later told a survey into the *blitz* experience.

Nora Norgate recalled:

'More high explosive and incendiary bombs fell, causing more fires and more loss of life but we were in the comparative safety of our Anderson shelter that night. Many people were so apprehensive that they left the city during the nights, sleeping in any kind of shelter available in the surrounding countryside and returned to their homes the following morning. During the next seven or eight days after those two air raids, our family would leave our home after tea, walk out of the city, carrying blankets, pillows, sandwiches, hot tea in flasks and our torches to the Mile Cross Bridge and sleep under the bridge each night. We were up early the following morning, walked home and then went to our various places of work. About 30 barrage balloons were installed around Norwich shortly after the two raids and in early May 1942 they proved their worth because here was another, larger air raid, but the bombs fell on the outskirts of the city.'

'During the next six or seven weeks which followed the Norwich 'blitz' continues Ted Harvey 'the Norwich and district division was reinforced with more personnel and appliances and once again were swept into action as a result of the thousands of incendiary bombs which fell on the City on the night of 26/27 June. Some of the bombing was extremely accurate and among the targets were the Cathedral, King Edward VII School, St. Paul and St. Michael-at-Thorn church, the Hebrew Community's Synagogue and St. Mary's Trinity Presbyterian church. The sheer weight of the number of calls meant that some of these targets became a total loss but in other cases the National Fire Service (NFS) personnel saved the day. Sharing in the glory must be the NFS women who manned the petrol tankers, the canteen vans and the mobile kitchens, not forgetting their colleagues who kept at their telephone posts when the buildings were rocking from the near-misses of falling bombs and last, but not least, the messenger lads who raced over the city on foot and cycle when telephones were 'out'. [John Grix, a 15-year old messenger boy had been blown off his bicycle five times by bombs as he pedalled between warden posts in the early hours of 30 April. Each time, he got back on and completed his journey. His remarkable bike ride earned him a British Empire Medal]. All of these would remember feeling quietly satisfied after a hectic night, having finished yet another duty period in their worthwhile job.'

Tyneside was apparently the German target on 30 April/1 May but several raiders roamed over East Anglia. At 4.12am about 700 incendiary bombs fell in Norwich and although fires were started no other aircraft bombed the city. The failure of the AA and night-fighter defences led to the deployment of 35 barrage balloons in and around Norwich. By 2 May all were in position and operational. The collective material effect on housing in the raids was severe; the Ministry of Home Security in a 'Top Secret' report on 6 May recorded '… 14,000 houses were damaged, of which 1,200 are wrecked'; 20 factories were either destroyed or seriously damaged.

Ted Harvey wrote that 'At the end of that week the firemen were almost 'out on their feet' but they would not have missed it for anything. The NFS Division 'A' of Fire Force 13 had been 'blooded'.

8/9 May 1942

This raid, had it been on target, would surely have been the most destructive of the war. German sources indicate that 76 aircraft set out and at least 40 crews were briefed to attack Norwich. The first bombers crossed the Norfolk coast at 12.40am and at 12.43 the first bombs began falling – but not in the city. A flare dropped by one of the first German bombers started a fire between two sites at the Chain Home radar station at Stoke Holy Cross (Poringland) and in the confusion that followed, the attack appears to have developed around this. Balloons were raised to 3,500 feet as a precautionary measure and later some were raised further as the attack progressed. At 1.04am with at least 16 enemy aircraft approaching the Norwich area from the East and NE the heavy AA gun batteries at Horsham St. Faith, Mousehold and Eaton opened fire. The 'Starfish' fire decoy site at Bramerton was ordered to ignite and during the next 40 minutes the parishes round the SE outskirts of the city received the full brunt of the enemy attack and 62 HE bombs fell near the radar station at Stoke Holy Cross, which however, remained operative throughout and sustained only slight damage. Adjoining Caister St. Edmund received 30 HE bombs, two parachute mines (the first time these weapons were used against an East Anglian target in these raids) and several thousand incendiary bombs, almost all falling in open fields. Poringland's share of the bombing was 30 HE bombs, two parachute mines and a 'large number' of incendiary bombs. In all, 180 HE bombs, ranging in size from 50 kg to 1000 kg, 8 parachute mines and at least 6,000 incendiary bombs (78 containers) dropped at 21 different locations in Norfolk that night. The composition of HE bomb types was far from clear owing to delayed-action bombs and the scattered nature of the attack but it was estimated that at least 51 x 250 kg, 53 x 500 kg and 14 x 1000 kg (plus 11 bombs of 'unspecified' size) had been used.

By 2am the raid was over. 75 tonnes of bombs including incendiaries had been dropped. It is unclear why the German attack misfired, whether this was due to the efforts of Balloon

Command, the decoys, or a combination of both, no-one knows. Out of 21 houses and premises hit by bombs, eight were completely destroyed and six badly damaged. Most of the damage done occurred at small villages and farms all round the City outskirts such as Thorpe, Salhouse, Swardeston, Heckingham, Marlingford and Runhall. Casualties outside the city amounted to two killed and six injured. Home Security noted that the only Key Point affected by the bombing was a railway line closed a quarter of a mile north of Wroxham railway station and the feature of this raid was the number of unexploded HE bombs used, many exploding unexpectedly during the days following. Weather conditions over Norwich itself were near perfect, with only 2/10ths cloud, no moon but bright starlight and although some raiders descended as low as 500 feet in the vicinity of Stoke Holy Cross, few appear to have braved the balloon barrage area. There were two exceptions. At 1.35am two 1000 kg bombs fell near the Woodlands Hospital. There was severe blast damage but no casualties from the only bombs to hit the city that night. Jack Wymer, a disabled boy of 11 recalled being bombed out at the old hospital (now West Norwich). 'Fire bombs had already hit the garage on Guardian Road. Anti-aircraft guns were banging away and shattered dormitory windows filled our beds with glass. Incendiaries also struck our building and smoke poured in at the bedroom door, which was ripped off its hinges by the blast. I heard despairing cries of fire victims before rescuers carried me on to mattresses outside. The night passed and I was evacuated to Gressenhall.'

Edward LeGrice was asked to make the photographic survey of the damage done. It provided him with an experience he believed to be unique among photographers. 'The Woodlands Hospital and especially the block of buildings used for the infirm and aged, had suffered terribly. To obtain evidence of certain happenings I had to climb high up and clamber over the shattered roofs. Not a pleasant task at such a height. I managed to get twelve pictures of the most striking scenes and by that time I had enough for one afternoon and so returned home to develop my films. To my utter astonishment when unwinding the backing paper, I was unable to find the film which should have been attached. As I always work without any light at all during developing operations, I tried again and again to find the film, but in vain and at last switched on a dim red light, only to find the film had been omitted from that particular spool. It was no light task to retrace my steps and retake all the pictures, but I managed to do it without any serious accident.' [157]

At 1.30am a Dornier 217E-4 of I/KG.2 at Gilze Rijen in Holland flown by Oberleutnant Werner Böllert flew into a balloon cable at Lakenham. The balloon was at 5,525 feet, flying over Site 33 at Long John's Hill, the Dornier at 3,500 feet. The sound of the impact was quite audible on the ground above the AA gunfire. The balloon fell to earth ablaze. The Dornier plunged towards the ground and was only able to recover at 200 feet. Crippled, it headed SE away from Norwich and flew straight into the fire of the light AA gun sites near Poringland. At least one eye-witness claims the German returned fire in a desperate exchange of tracers before finally crashing in a meadow at West Poringland where it burst into flames. Böllert and his crew of three were killed instantly. They were laid to rest in Norwich Cemetery, Earlham.

On 9 May a German broadcast claimed that: 'All that remained was an enormous heap of ruins'. After a lull, the *Baedeker* offensive resumed with Hull as the target on the night of 19/20 May.

26/27 June 1942

The 'Alert' sounded at 2.05am on a brilliantly moonlit Saturday morning. With 12 mile visibility and only sporadic AA fire and searchlights, thirty raiders made a determined attempt to raze Norwich to the ground. Balloons were raised well in advance and remained at 6,500 feet. At 2.10am flares ignited NW of Norwich and the assault began. While casualties were proportionately light (16 killed and 70 persons injured – 15 of these serious hospital cases) some devastating fires resulted and defied the reorganised and reinforced Fire Service in this, the last of the *Luftwaffe*'s major raids on Norwich. This was the largest fire-bomb raid mounted against an East Anglian target in WW2, remembered as the 'firebomb blitz'. Only 33 HE bombs (11 tonnes) were reported, but something like 9½ tonnes of incendiary bombs were dropped and for the first time the Cathedral was hit. Although some bombers flew as low as 300 feet elsewhere, there was clear evidence of the height forced on the enemy crews by the balloon barrage, most remaining at about 8,000 feet. So many incendiaries rained down on districts in the space of 35 minutes that no accurate count was ever apparently made. The Air Warfare Analysis Section of the RAF made an initial conservative estimate of 8,597 but Police reports following the raid make it quite clear that the true figure was much higher; at least 15,000 and possibly as many as 20,000 individual fire-bombs. Norwich air raid historian Norman Bacon recalled:

'Many places were left to burn themselves out – Horns Lane School, a shop in King Street, St. Michael-at-Thorn Church and Morgan's Brewery in King Street the fire service was overwhelmed and the mobile fire column took hours to reach Norwich. Burleigh Street was simply littered with incendiaries the next morning, both burnt out and UXB, although the Fire Watch Party had saved all the houses.' Major fires raged at Thorpe Station, Colegate, Magdalen Street, Muspole Street and at the Carrow Works, to mention a few. At least 1,500 incendiaries failed to ignite, either having fallen in unopened containers, in soft ground, or bounced off buildings without detonating. Dozens of bombs of several different types were still being found by souvenir hunting schoolboys months after the raid.

Trevor Castleton, nearly nine years old, recalled:

'We were living with my grandparents in St. John Street off Rose Lane and I was a pupil at Horns Lane School. Already we'd had several raids on the city. Our street had been hit and the 'Orchard Tavern' on the corner of Mountergate had been destroyed [on 2 December 1940]. Once I was in the playground at Horns Lane when we heard a plane diving straight at us. We all rushed to the air-raid shelter next to St. Julian's churchyard. While I was still some distance away from the shelter one of my plimsolls came off and like a 'duzy fule' I stopped to pick it up. By then the plane was directly above me firing its machine guns. It was so low I could see the crew. I stood rooted to the spot, watching fascinated as it flashed over.

'We had an Anderson shelter in our back yard. My sister and I spent many horrible nights in it. It was always damp and cold. Sometimes I'd wake up during the night to find one of my old aunts had crawled in because of a raid. There was a brick surface shelter at the back of our houses and that's where we were on the first night of the Blitz. These shelters had four cell-like compartments, each one allocated to two houses. They contained two sets of double bunks. During the raid the din was horrendous and seemed to go on for hours. Some of the explosions sounded really close, the ground rocked and we feared our house would be hit. I don't remember being scared; in fact I tried to go out and watch but was dragged back and given a clip round the ear. A neighbour said the whole city was on fire. In my childish ignorance I was quite excited. I remember hoping that my school would get hit. It eventually did! We emerged from the shelter in the morning and everybody looked automatically towards the Cathedral. It was still standing.

'After the second raid me and a pal went into the city and looked at the damage. We ran up over the cattle market and could hear the bells of fire engines and ambulances coming from Castle Meadow way. The sky was still thick with smoke and as we got close to Golden Ball Street it was obvious that a lot of bombs had fallen around Ber Street and All Saints' Green. The biggest shock met us at the bottom of Timber Hill. Orford Place, which had been an area of big shops like Bunting's, Curls and Woolworth's, was just a huge heap of rubble. All those buildings were completely gutted. The stench was unforgettable, a mixture of dust, soot and burning wood.'

Arthur Whittingham, senior fireguard in charge of The Close and surveyor to the Dean and Chapter during the war, recalls that 'Norwich Cathedral was fortunate during the war in having slight damage early on [on 2 December 1940]; enough to alert people to the dangers, so that by the time of the more serious attacks in 1942, precautions had been taken. However, had there been a high wind or a direct hit the results could easily have been worse. Early in 1941, after consultation, improvements were made in access to the upper parts of the Cathedral so that there was a complete circulation way at different levels with casements on to the roofs and external ladders, ways across were formed on the organ loft and through the nave roof. At strategic points, sandbags, pails, water and stirrup pumps were placed. The belfry and spire windows were blocked to prevent the tower acting as a flue. Three fire-watching posts were provided for the whole Close, one in the Cathedral tower at roof level and the others at the top of the tallest office building in the upper and the lower square of the Close. Each was manned by a paid watcher and a rota of volunteers from offices; residents and the school, the scheme being compulsory for offices and organisations of a certain size. As senior fireguard for the Close, as well as in charge of repairs for the Dean and Chapter, it was convenient for the writer to live in Bishopgate in the three raids at the end of April, 1942; the only trouble in the Close was a high explosive on the 30th in the playing field next to the allotments. This broke glass and brought down pantiles from the roofs, into the gutters of 70 houses in the Close. Fortunately, rain held off during the next few weeks while the roofs were being repaired, but for several weeks pigeons were flying through the Cathedral.

'The real test was on 27 June 1942. After a 2am siren came the drone of planes followed by the brilliant pink light from chandeliers floating slowly down. As Canon Clayton reached the high east roof of the Cathedral, the firewatcher from the tower, Mr. A. G. Saunders, remarked he, was expecting trouble. Approaching from north-west, planes dropped high explosives, then incendiaries. Our anti-aircraft guns were firing. As high explosives fell nearer, Mr. Saunders felt it was time to ring the headmaster's warning bell in the school crypt. Soon after there was Mr. Acland in the nave calling up that he had two boys ready (nine more without helmets were kept back till the planes had passed and firing had stopped). A plane came in low over the Maid's Head dropping incendiaries. He and his boys, joined by a few other people put out one in the science block and those on the sheds and arcade, with sand, buckets, and stirrup-pumps for those stuck in the roof. They were still doing this when flames burst through the west part of the adjoining lodge roof, which had already been burning fiercely inside and unseen; so that all they could do when they reached the entrance was rescue equipment from the ground floor.

'One boy, J. F. Watson, was just going in when he heard the whine of another large container coming down from a second plane, perhaps ten minutes after the first. It burst on impact, burning up harmlessly among the scatter of incendiaries already in the playground. Watching from the lower square, my first objective was to see what had happened to the Cathedral. There was obviously something behind the nave roof near the tower, where I found the watcher and two others coping with an incendiary in the triforium roof. More serious, a fire was just beginning to burn through the north transept roof (it was found eventually that a container of 42 incendiaries had wedged in a pocket of the vaulting) and had gained a strong hold. So the watcher whistled up Mr. Jack Woolsey with his National Fire Service trailer-pump from Palace Plain. He kept this fire under control, while using his second hose to put out two fires in opposite corners of the palace roof. Canon Green put out a small fire in the south transept roof from the window above after Mr. Hardy the gate porter, complaining of 'them incinders' had tackled it from inside the roof. Thin reinforced concrete had saved the north part of the organ, but an adjoining small fire from the incendiary above could have caused trouble.

'Two incendiaries had bounced along the south triforium and burst up ineffectually but one over the Bauchun chapel and another over St. Luke's were more tiresome. Messrs. Overton, Scales and Webster dealt with some of these. The trailer went on to two other fires, one in the Monastic Infirmary (Houses 63, Mr. Stefan Cooke and 66, Dr. Preston) the remains of which were destroyed except for the pillars in the car park and the other in the two offices east of the upper square (67 and 68) part of 67 being burnt out where the hoses prevented the fires spreading. On the west of this square the offices (71 and 75) each had an incendiary in the roof put out with difficulty and the same applies to 51, at the east end of the Monastic granary along the north side of the lower square where Miss Doyle was busy. Though the raid was over before 3am there was still much work to be done before breakfast; and the canister in the transept roof burned for 14 hours. This and 30 incendiaries caused fire, but the majority of perhaps 800 in the Close burnt out harmlessly on the ground or on hard surfaces; or failed to ignite.'

The HE bombs dropped comprised; 22 x 250 kg; 9 x 500 kg; 1 x 1000 kg and one HE bomb of 'unclassified' size. It was estimated that 66% of the total bomb tonnage carried had found Norwich. For once the Germans were not exaggerating when they claimed: 'Reconnaissance planes brought back accurate pictures of the havoc wrought by last night's attack. It was confirmed that extensive fires had ravaged the target area.' In addition to 2,500 houses being affected, two factories and one railway goods yard were hit and in all, 663 fires started.

On 27/28 July the *Luftwaffe* launched the first of three consecutive raids on Birmingham using virtually every available bomber in the west. Instructor crews and even crews trained in torpedo-dropping in III/KG.26 were used in the attack. There was also an unusual raid on Norwich at 12.20am by one aircraft variously identified as a He 111, Do 217 or Ju 88. In the balloon-defended area the German machine sent one balloon flaming earthwards and then narrowly missed colliding with a second cable before escaping into the darkness. Two 'Flam 500' incendiary Bomb Containers scattered 240 fire-bombs in a straight line between Pottergate and Coslany Street, starting fires which were soon dealt with. One 1000 kg HE bomb from the same aircraft fell near Trafford Road, where it blasted a 90-foot wide crater in an orchard and damaged 40 houses. Amazingly, no casualties resulted.

1/2 August 1942

At 2.12am sirens again sounded in Norwich and raid lasting about 30 minutes was made by 20 aircraft, mostly Do 217s flying at 9,000 feet and above, out of the balloon barrage area. Flares once more ignited and this time 5,000 incendiaries, about one third of which were the new steel-nosed explosive variety. This weapon, a larger version of the 1 kg fire-bombs, contained anti-personnel charge in the nose. Armed during descent, the explosive charge detonated 4½ minutes (or less) after impact, released from altitude the incendiary bombs in this attack impacted at high speed, some going 8½ feet into soft earth. Others smashed through the roofs of buildings and shelters to burn and explode inside. Despite an almost continuous barrage of AA fire including 487 UP rockets, further flares were dropped and after a brief pause, more raiders unloaded their bombs. Among the 38 fires reported were incidents in Duke Street, Magdalen Street, Heigham Street and Barrack Street. Mixed in with the fire-bombs were a few HEs, including a 1000 kg bomb, which blasted a gaping 69-feet-wide crater in Branford Road. Further HE bombs fell in the river near the Water Works; on Clarkes Boot Factory (burned out in a previous raid) one in Old Palace Road (six houses wrecked) and in Sprowston Road. Several air-raid shelters were hit by bombs and although many people had extraordinary escapes, five people – including a one-week-old child – were killed; 27 were injured. Bombs also fell at Sprowston, Trowse, Spixworth and Ketteringham that night. Raid-spotter Mr. Edwin J. Comber recorded: 'The Air Raid Message 'White' at 03.19 hours saw fires and desolation spread throughout the city.' Security reported: 'Substantial damage to commercial and domestic property.' In all, 8.20 tonnes of bombs hit Norwich, or 79.25% of the total carried.

13/14 August 1942

Continuing the reduced scale of bombing effort over Britain, 16 enemy aircraft set out for Norwich yet again, in what was to prove the Parthian shaft of the 1942 *Baedeker* night raids against the battered but still defiant city. Sirens sounded at 10.41pm in Norwich and a vigorous barrage of AA gunfire greeted the visitors. Flares which ignited North and NW of the city centre were in turn fired on by the guns in an attempt to destroy the parachutes. Balloons were again raised well in advance and the defenders were successful in that only five bombers crossed the city area and only one managed to place its load within the Norwich boundaries. At 11.17pm an ABB 500 container and three HE bombs fell in the Mousehold area. The incendiary bombs from the container started one fire in Catton Grove Road. The HE bombs of 500kg (1,110lb) size blew large craters in the ground; one on allotments near Gertrude Road, one in the grounds of Mousehold Avenue Infants School and one harmlessly on heath land. The German bombers, flying at about 8,000 feet, also dropped at Thorpe (1 person injured), Kirby Bedon (1,000 incendiaries), on RAF Horsham St. Faith (360 incendiaries) and at Sprowston (1 person injured) and Great Plumstead. By midnight the raiders had departed, leaving 50 Norwich houses damaged but no one injured in the city itself. Fighter Command thought 15 bombers had been involved, approaching at heights of between 10,000-15,000 feet and then losing altitude to 5,000 feet after crossing the coast. They also reported incendiary fires causing some damage to stacks and crops in Norfolk during this raid. No enemy aircraft were lost.

The last *Baedeker* raid of any size aimed at East Anglia was mounted on King's Lynn on 17/18 September 1942 by just nine Do 217 bombers of KG2 that took off from Deelen airfield in Holland at 8.14pm. At the briefing crews were instructed to simply aim their bomb loads at the centre of the town. The alternative target was Great Yarmouth but in fact, no bombs fell there. Thus ended the *Baedeker* reprisal raids against targets in Norfolk and Suffolk. Norwich had suffered more than 220 fatalities during the two April 1942 raids alone and the damage took years to repair. Other cities had suffered even worse in the 14 main *Baedeker* raids but the cost to the enemy had been 40 aircraft; flown by some of their most experienced aircrews. An excerpt from *Norwich Under Fire* by George Swain states: 'By the end of 1944 we had more than 1,450 alerts, 670 HE bombs and 25,000 incendiary bombs: 330 of us had been killed and 1,100 wounded: 30,000 homes had been damaged, more than 2,000 of them beyond repair.'

Over a month elapsed before a further serious onslaught was made and in the first week in August a new type of incendiary with an explosive charge was used, resulting in five deaths and again in September a minor attack masked the fact that the crisis was over. By October Allied forces were taking the offensive, the *Luftwaffe*, having failed to intimidate, as it failed to destroy Norwich, had other more urgent tasks on hand. From this date, only occasional small scale raids took place. On 18 March 1943 the Alert sounded at 22.30 hours. Enemy aircraft then proceeded to release sixty SBC 50 incendiaries (a spring-band type containing a cluster of small incendiary units and a 12lb explosive charge) and a number of phosphorus bombs on Norwich. One of the phosphorus bombs hit Harmer's large clothing factory in St. Andrews and most of the original factory was gutted by fire, which threatened the new Telephone Exchange opposite. Harmer's (founded in 1825) had been attacked in previous raids and each time production was maintained at seven different addresses. It was now engaged on Government contracts for the supply of uniforms to the Armed Forces and Civil Defence, just as it had in World War I when in 1915 its production had been two tons of uniforms daily. [192/3] Three more minor raids on Norwich occurred but that of 6 November 1943 was the last attack on the city. It was the 44th raid on Norwich by the *Luftwaffe*. From that date on enemy air activity was to be confined to occasional reconnaissance flights. The total number of Alerts during 1943 was 95 with a total duration of 54 hours. The Crash Warning was sounded 50 times with a total duration of 19 hours 8½ minutes.

On 26 June 1944 a new terror weapon, the *Vergeltungswaffe 1* (Revenge Weapon No. 1), or Fieseler Fi 103 *Kirschkern* (Cherry Stone), a small pilotless aircraft with a 1,870lb high explosive warhead, which detonated on impact, was seen over Norwich for the first time. The anticipated 'rocket blitz' had had been delayed by problems until 13 June when ten V-1s were catapult-launched at London from sites in north-eastern France. The British press dubbed the fearsome weapon 'Doodlebug'. At night the V-1s the long tail of exhaust gases glowed in the sky. 'Ossy' Osbiston recalls:

'If my memory serves me right, actually only three V-1s were dropped on the city. One fell on the marsh opposite Thorpe St. Andrew Church. This one damaged the clock and the stone spire twisting it from the base of the spire and tower. This was replaced after operations on prefabricated lines and lowered. [At 6.10pm on 26 September a very loud explosion was heard which seemed to come from the direction of Ranworth but no information could be obtained as to its origin. Then at 10.55am the next day another explosion occurred north of the City and later that day two more were heard, one from the general direction of Great Yarmouth and the other from the Bramerton area. At no time was any sign of a missile seen or heard.] Some large industrial buildings were extensively damaged or knocked completely out, for instance Caley Mackintosh, Colman's on Bracondale and King Street. The Cathedral north and south transept roof timbers and lead were burned off and all stained glass windows were either smashed or buckled. A large amount of stone tracery had to be replaced.'

On 29 September there was an explosion at Coltishall followed by one at Whitlingham. Again on 3 October 1944 at 7.45pm the whole City was shaken by a large detonation and superficial blast damage to property in the Mile Cross and Dereham Road areas was reported. On the north side of Hellesdon Golf Course debris from a missile was strewn over an area of 600 yards and a shallow crater 4 feet deep and 32 by 27 feet wide supplemented the bunkers on the course. An ARP report referred to this missile as 'Big Ben' or the V-2 rocket. Fate decreed that none should fall within the city boundaries. In 1944 the Alert sounded 76 times covering a total time of 42 hours 22 minutes.

Pippa Miller recalled that 'Before the war ended the 'Doodlebugs' [V-1 rockets] arrived. From a window of our flat facing east we could see the searchlights and tracer bullets as these flying bombs crossed the coast at Lowestoft. Anxiously we watched, because if their course was straight towards you, you were probably safe – because they always turned aside before they descended. At another time we were instructed in the behaviour of the latest German weapon to be launched at us – the small 'butterfly' or anti-personnel bombs. They fell in clusters and were designed to catch on any projection – a tree, a gutter, a telephone wire or fence – and the next time they were vibrated by a passing vehicle or pedestrian they would explode.

'My last recollection of the war years in Norwich is quite different from all the rest. It concerns feeling hungry and tightening one's belt. Toward the end of the conflict, two of us went to a 'safe' area of the country for a short break. Our hotel naturally took and used our ration books to feed us.

'After one long day's tramp in the countryside, revelling in the freedom from fear, we were famished. So we called in the little village shop and begged for something, anything, to eat. But there was nothing – even bread and potatoes were rationed then. In fact, we would even have welcomed dog biscuits!'

On 8 May 1945 war in Europe ended. Early buses carried workers who were in some doubt as to the time the Victory in Europe Holiday Celebrations were to begin, so they went to work to find out. At 9am at Britannia Barracks a thousand Servicemen attended a drumhead service and were then given the rest of the day off to join in the general celebrations, but at this point nobody seemed to know what form these celebrations were to take. With children in mind many street parties were being arranged.

In the ruins of St. Mary's Baptist Chapel on St. Mary's Plain, which was destroyed in the raids of 1942, the rubble was swept away and a few seats put out and a Thanksgiving Service was held. That night American Liberators and RAF Mosquitoes flying overhead dropped scores of coloured flares and were caught in the searchlights which continually swept the city skies. By midnight the crowds were ecstatic with happiness.

Some of the ancient churches were ruined but generally, the old stone buildings of Norwich withstood the effect of blast and the famous Norman Castle and Cathedral bore few marks of the City's ordeal. Post-war evidence reveals that British intelligence knew shortly before each attack the area to be targeted, but defensive measures proved lamentably weak in the face of a well-mounted and accurate assault. Of the city's 35,569 houses in 1939, 2,082 were destroyed entirely, 2,651 were seriously damaged and 25,621 were moderately damaged. In human toll 340 people were killed and 1,092 injured, over three-quarters of these casualties occurring in 1942.

The Auxiliary Fire Service and their converted saloon cars outside Bethel Street just before the war. They were severely tested as Norwich became the target for some of the heaviest air raids of the Second World War.

German target map of Norwich in 1939 which was still in use in 1941.

Sandbags are positioned on the steps of the City Hall. William Joyce who was better known as 'Lord Haw Haw' had a special message for Norwich when he announced on German radio that 'The people of Norwich have a new City Hall. It isn't paid for yet. But never mind, the *Luftwaffe* will soon put said to it ...' The traitor's boast fortunately never came true.

Bethel Street Police and Fire Station in Bethel Street which was built in 1934 was split into two separate services in 1941. Note the fire helmets in relief above the doorway.

Fire drill at Bethel Street Fire Station.

British citizens erected Anderson shelters in their back gardens and Morrison shelters in their homes as protection against air attack. Anderson shelters were one of the greatest helps provided by the Government for the safeguarding of the people during air raids. These shelters not only saved many lives, but were of the greatest value in maintaining morale. They gave a sense of security which enabled many people to stand up to the bombing not only during the *blitz*, but also during the many warnings of the approach of enemy aircraft.

Mrs. Clementine Churchill and Herbert Morrison, who in the winter of 1940 replaced Sir John Anderson as Home Secretary, visiting a home to see a Morrison shelter – a reinforced table which provided protection except against direct hits – in operation.

A gardener in Dereham Road camouflaged his Anderson shelter so that it was an adornment instead of an eyesore. He spent many hours gathering waste and broken bricks with which he surrounded his shelter, supported the protecting soil and then planted it with various rock plants and thus transformed it into a thing of beauty.

The Steward family at 80 Bull Close Road (Fred Steward is perched on one of the bottom floor windows) had a lucky escape on 19 July 1940 when a lone bomber dropped seven HE bombs in the Botolph Street, Pitt Street, St. George Street and Magdalen Street areas of the city in Raid 2 at 0600 hours. Nos. 20, 22 and 24 Bull Close and the rear of the 'Cat & Fiddle' pub were hit. Two civilians were injured.

Black out curtains which were put up in every house and factory premises in Britain after war broke out in 1939.

A wrecked bus at the Surrey Street Bus Station after Raid 3 by a Do 215Z at 0600 hours on Tuesday 30 July 1940. In all, twenty 50 kg HE bombs were dropped and these fell at Arthur St. Nursing Home, the Bus Station, King St. by Read's Mill, Horns Lane, Compass St by Argyle St., Printing dept at Carrow Works, Market Gardens, Sandy Lane; Compass St by Mariners Lane and Victoria Terrace. Fourteen people were killed, including Mrs Phyllis Bramble (26) and her 17-month old baby and two children aged 3 and 5 at 6 Victoria Terrace. At No.14 all four members of the Johnson family died. Twenty-seven people were injured. Again, there was no 'alert' before this raid took place. One of the Royal Engineers involved was Lieutenant Ian Hoare, a Norwich man. In all, four bombs fell at 0055/0100 hours; two were oil IBs, which fell in heath land at Long Valley, Mousehold, one was a DA HE which exploded 12 hours later.

George Swain photographed the removal by block and tackle of the time sensitive SC500 (1,110lb) HE UXB, which had smashed through the path and embedded itself 30 ft into the soft subsoil outside No. 4 Theatre Street on the night of Wednesday 18/19 September 1940 (Raid 7). The men from 8 Section, No. 4 Bomb Disposal Company, Royal Engineers arrived on 24 September. They knew the device could detonate anything up to 96 hours after it was dropped and even the slightest movement could start the clockwork fuse ticking again. It took a total of four days to uncover and defuse the bomb. Having been made safe the bomb was then loaded onto an army lorry and was removed to Harford tip. In December 1940 three men in the bomb disposal team received the award of the George Medal, which was introduced on 24 September 1940.

Workmen begin the task of clearing up amid the rubble of the 'Orchard Tavern' in Mountergate on the morning of Tuesday 3 December 1940 after a single bomber (probably a Do 17Z) scattered bombs through a blanket of fog at tea-time on Monday 2 December (Raid 12). One bomb demolished the front of the 'Orchard Tavern'. Incredibly, the licensee and his family escaped unhurt.

On the evening of Monday 2 December 1940 in the 12th air raid on Norwich six people were killed and five injured (two seriously) in St. John Street in the wreckage of three cottages – Nos. 43, 45 and 47 – which were destroyed. ARP Wardens helped the Rescue Party in helping people free themselves. A police special was killed by bomb blast in Bracondale.

Morgan's Brewery in Synagogue Street, which was gutted on 2 December 1940. Three soldiers walking past saw beer flowing past them.

Salvaging what possessions they can, people pick through the ruins of two houses in King Street on 3 December 1940.

UXB in King Street.

On Carrow Hill on the morning of Wednesday 11 December 1940 William Warnes (83) who was in bed, was blown into the front garden of his cottage at 10 The Vale when a bomb exploded at the bottom of the hill. Incredibly, Mr. Warnes, who had refused to sleep downstairs along with his daughter Kate and 18-year old grand-daughter Eileen Gertrude, was unhurt. His daughter was injured but survived but his grand-daughter was killed.

Carrow Hill street sign. On Tuesday 9 July 1940, a bomb crashed through trees at the top of the hill near the Black Tower and exploded at ground level as women leaving work at Colman's were pushing their bicycles up the hill. Two women were killed instantly and three later died of their injuries.

Part of a Norwich scout group collecting waste-paper.

Norwich schoolchildren collecting scrap metal.

A young boy picks through the rubble in Rupert Street.

A mobile YMCA canteen serves food and hot drinks to people clearing up the debris in Walpole Street after the raid on 17/18 February 1941 (Raid 16) when 140 people were made homeless, among them Leslie 'George' Hatch, a Royal Navy stoker on destroyers (far right of the group) who obtained compassionate leave to move his wife and 6-year old son Tony and sister Janice (his wife Dorothy is 4th from right) to George Pope Road at Catton Grove after their house was destroyed. This, the 17th raid of the war, began shortly before midnight and both sides of Vauxhall Street from Nos. 40 to 60 and Nos. 45 to 51 were wrecked. Many more damaged in the surrounding area. One very large HE bomb fell from a Heinkel He 111 at 0455 hours (one account says 0505 hours) in Vauxhall Street. The damage was serious and also included houses badly damaged in Horace Street, Walpole Street and Coach and Horses Street. Casualties were eight killed and 20 injured. It is quite possible that the bomb was an SC 1800 'Satan' dropped by a He 111 of III/KG.26 in a solo Y-System attack on Norwich.

The NFS (National Fire Service) was kept busy on the night of Tuesday 29/30 April 1941, as bombs caused widespread devastation in the industrial heart of Norwich. No.17 City Road was demolished by blast, which also caused extensive damage to adjoining properties and a gas-main was demolished. The raid began at 2210 hours on 29 April. The bombs included 11 HEs, some of which had B1E1 IBs wired onto the tail fins and five of which were UXBs, approximately 100 IBs plus about 30 which did not ignite, and several oil IBs. Small fires were caused by IBs at the premises of Boulton Paul and Laurence, Scott & Electromotors Ltd. Casualties were two killed and 11 injured.

King Street after 30 April 1941.

A wrecked corner shop in King Street on Wednesday 30 April 1941.

A wrecked corner shop in King Street on Wednesday 30 April 1941.

Workmen try to repair a bomb crater in Exchange Street.

Exchange Street with church of St. John Maddermarket behind.

The bomb which fell on 47 Cadge Close around midnight on Wednesday 7 May 1941 killed Mr Edward Joseph Britcher (41), his wife Ethel (37) and three children aged 10, 13 and 15. Three more children were seriously injured when the house collapsed on them and they were later dug out by a rescue squad. The blast from this bomb also damaged roofs and bedrooms of neighbouring houses. Next door the Robinson family had a remarkable escape when all seven members suffered only superficial injuries although two of the boys were buried beneath the rubble of their home. Five bombs in all fell in the gardens of this road causing considerable damage. The Larkman Lane area bore the brunt of this, the 25th raid of the war. Twenty-two (or 24, reports differ) 50 kg HE bombs were dropped, 150 people were made homeless, five people were killed and 30 were injured.

A schoolboy stands among the wreckage of Blenheim IV Z7275 of 139 Squadron which crashed immediately after take-off from Horsham St Faith (now Norwich Airport) on a night training flight at 2104 hours on 22 November 1941. The aircraft hit a house on the Brabazon Road junction with Cromer Road and four houses were set on fire. There were five civilian casualties; two of which were taken to hospital, three with shock. The pilot, P/O Russell Scott-Worthington, was killed, P/O David Carl Taylor the observer died from his injuries the next day. (He is buried in Norwich). Sergeant J. Koller the WOp/AG was injured. He was later killed on ops on 21 'Norwich' Squadron in 1943.

Dornier Do 17Z U5+EA of Stab/KG.2 which was brought down by AA gunfire on Friday, 23 August 1940 and belly-landed in a clover field at Lodge Farm, Wickhambrook, Suffolk, on display in Eaton Park, Norwich. The crew of four survived and were taken prisoner.

Blazing shops in St Stephen's Street 27/28 April 1942.

Flames light up the sky during the raid of 27/28 April which resulted in an inferno engulfing 120 acres, silhouetting the tower of St. Lawrence's Church.

Bomb damage next to the Theatre Royal.

Along Bethel Street towards St. Giles.

City Maternity Home on Earlham Road.

City Station.

Burned out carriages beneath the skeletal remains of the platform canopy at City Station.

City Station.

Westwick Street.

The flames from the Coleman's Wincarnis Works, Westwick Street were so intense they scorched George Swain's camera when he took this photograph on the night of 29/30 April 1942.

Westwick Street after the 29/30 April 1942 bombing *blitz*.

Fight nerves,
worry, fatigue with

THE QUICK ACTION TONIC

Wincarnis is putting new heart and life into thousands of women who were feeling 'just a bit down.' For war-time nerviness and general over-strain, there is no substitute for the quick restorative action of Wincarnis. You can *feel* the strength flowing into you, from the fine continental wines reinforced with beef and malt extracts.
BUY WINCARNIS NOW. THE PRICE IS NOT YET UP, IN SPITE OF THE NEW WINE DUTY.

X A NURSE'S TESTIMONIAL—
'I am just recovering from an attack of bronchitis, have found it a good pick-me-up. I shall certainly have more, and recommend it to my patients.' Nurse V.K. (Cornwall)

Health is priceless

WINCARNIS

Still only 5'6 and 3'3

Wincarnis advertisement.

The City Corporation Depot in Westwick Street. James Davison (50), the staff officer of the City Rescue Squad at the depot was killed on the night of 27/28 April 1942 when a bomb exploded as he went to check on his injured men. His wife Ethel ran the corner shop at 71 Hotblack Road. Cecil George Lamb, a 49 year firewatcher, also died.

The remains of Bullard's Mineral Water Works on Westwick Street, just across from the City Corporation Depot after the raid on 27/28 April 1942.

Looking towards St. John's Roman Catholic cathedral from Westwick Street.

Collapsed roof of the main office of Norwich Union Insurance Society.

The Dolphin public house, formerly the palace of Bishop Joseph Hall 1571-1656, Bishop of Norwich from 1611 until 1617 when he was forced to retire after his cathedral had been pillaged and desecrated. It was desecrated again during the first of the *Baedeker* raids on Norwich on 27/28 April 1942. Nearby, on the corner of Raynham Street, 14 people sheltering in a surface air-raid shelter were killed when it received a direct hit. The 'Dolphin' has since been restored to its former glory.

Aerial view of Waterworks Road as it is today. (Author)

Waterworks Road street sign. (Author)

Aerial view of the Water works as it is today. (Author)

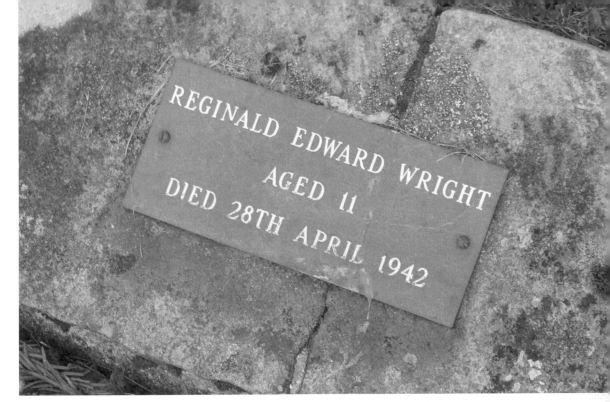

Memorial tablet to Reginald Wright (11) in the Garden of Remembrance at Earlham Cemetery, Norwich. He was killed along with his grandparents on the night of 27/28 April 1942. (Author)

Margaret Winifred Lockwood (3 months); Jack Reginald Lockwood (7); Beryl Kathleen Lockwood (11); Hilda May Lockwood, housewife (37) all killed at 65 Rosebery Road, Norwich on the night of 27/28 April 1942 are among those commemorated at the Garden of remembrance, Earlham Cemetery. (Author)

Recent aerial view of Little Armes Street. Today there are no houses on one side of Little Armes Street (off the bend in Waterworks Road, top, lined by trees and a factory is now on the site). At the former No.10 Little Armes Street 38-year old Donald Wilfred White, a milk roundsman and his 38 year old wife, Bessie Louisa also died on 27 April 1942.(Author)

Rupert Street, which was hit by bomb blast on the nights of 27/28 and 29/30 April 1942. At No.19 61-year old Mary Ellen Faulkner and Florence Elizabeth Gaze (59) and 70-year old Alice Rebecca Tuttle, a retired wool shop keeper, died. At No.25 72-year old Lucretia Lydia Freeman and 70-year old Jessie Maria Galey; a retired clothing works finisher, were killed. All four houses in Eagle Passage were destroyed. At Wellington Terrace and at Albert, Bixfields and Ellwoods Buildings, many of the devastated properties had to be demolished. At No.2 Bixfield Buildings 62-year old Arthur Butcher, a barman and his 62-year old wife Beatrice Louisa were killed. At No.3, 50-year old Daisy Ames, and her 81-year old widowed mother Ellen died. At No.6 80-year old Emily Maria Hewitt and at No.7 65-year old Rebecca Plummer, a domestic daily help, both died. At No.11 73-year old Emma Williamson died. So too did 70-year old Ada Eliza Clarke at No.12.

Nelson Street Schools on 30 April 1942.

Heigham House in West Parade off Earlham Road. One house in West Parade was destroyed and almost 20 more damaged by the blast from a single high explosive bomb during the *Baedeker* raids in April 1942.

Bury Street off Unthank Road.

Norfolk & Norwich Hospital.

Fire fighting near St. Andrew's Hall.

NFS firemen wearing breathing apparatus.

Women firefighters on the roof of a large shop in Orford Place.

Wrecked houses on Oak Street. On the night of 27/28 April 1942 a bomb that exploded in Oak Street wounded fireman Len Strivens and Malcolm Pease and killed Senior Company Officer NFS Sam Bussey, a 39-year old father of two who was trying to save some horses from blazing stables near Oak Street at the height of the raging inferno. He was the only full-time, regular police officer turned fireman to be killed during the Norwich *Blitz*. At 25 Esdelle Street Fred Garner (50) known as the 'mad barber' though he never cut hair but only sold wood from his yard in Oak Street – also died.

Norwich Fire Station in Bethel Street, which was built in 1934. At the time of the April *Blitz* Sam Bussey lived in Flat 4 with his wife Norah Mary Bussey. Three other officers and their families lived in the other flats. (Author)

Wartime Memorial tablet in the inner courtyard at Scholars Court on Oak Street inscribed '1942 Blitz' with Winston Churchill's V-for-Victory sign. (Author)

Military personnel beginning the clean up in Oak Street. The 'Buck' pub was wrecked while the 'White Lion' pub and the old Empire cinema were severely hit.

Above and opposite The 'Boar's Head', which had stood at the corner of Surrey Street since the 15th Century was destroyed.

View from the 'Boar's Head' towards St. Stephen's Church and the spire of St. Peter Mancroft.

Looking across the rooftops and the remains of the 'Boar's Head' to Caley's after much rubble had been cleared.

Caley's chocolate factory (later Rowntree Mackintosh) was one of the worst-hit buildings on the night of 29/30 April 1942. A blaze, fanned by a strong west wind, took a hold on the nearby Cuthbert's printing works and Caley's own fire brigade used its independent water supply to try and prevent the flames reaching their factory but Cuthbert's was gutted and when the fire spread to Caley's the water supply was exhausted. The two main buildings, which had been stacked with 1,000 tons of finished chocolates and stores of cardboard boxes, were completely burned out.

Caley's.

Caley's.

The remains of Caley's chocolate factory on 1 May 1942

On the night of Monday 27/28 April 1942 four 500kg HE bombs fell on Chapel Field Gardens, two of them direct hits upon the underground air raid shelter. Fortunately one of these failed to explode and was defused at 7.00am the following morning. Meanwhile the rescue of many of those who were trapped in the wreckage of the bombed shelter carried on regardless.

Bomb damage in Red Lion Street and Rampant Horse Street, April 1942.

Bomb damage in St. Stephen's Street.

A few bewildered people make their way through the bomb-damaged remains of Orford Place as the Emergency services douse the fires and clear up the devastation near the corner of Bunting's department store.

Firemen continue their work outside the burnt out shell of Bunting's store on Rampant Horse Street after the raid of 29/30 April 1942.

Hoses snake through the rubble-strewn city centre on Thursday 30 April as firemen toil in St. Stephen's Plain and Rampant Horse Street after the blaze the night before had destroyed Curls, Woolworth's and Bunting's among neighbouring businesses.

Orford Place after the blitz in April 1942.

Orford Place on the morning after the raid on 29/30 April.

Reflections in the emergency water pool on the ruined site of the Curls department store, which was cleared after being destroyed in the April bombing and a concrete basin was made and filled with 270,000 gallons of water to become a static tank for the use of fire appliances in the event of future raids. The church of St. Stephen is on the left and the Haymarket cinema is on the right.

Rampant Horse Street.

Rubble strewn Rampant Horse Street and devastated buildings as seen from St. Stephen's Church on the morning of Thursday 30 April.

Corner of Rampant Horse Street.

Workmen cleaning up in Orford Place.

NFS firemen damp down the still-smouldering debris in the ruins of Curls department store at the junction of Red Lion Street and Rampant Horse Street after the raid on Wednesday 29/30 April 1942.

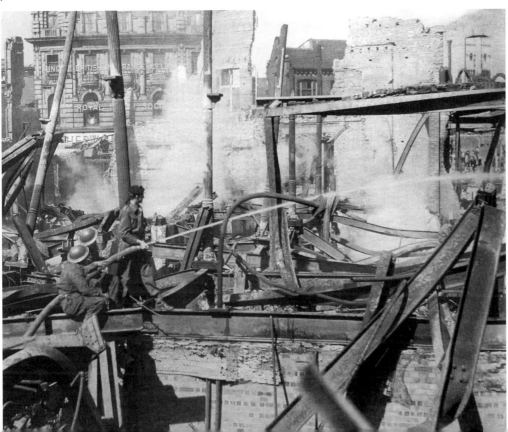

Clearing up in St. Stephen's Street, looking towards Queen's Road.

St. Stephen's Plain and Rampant Horse Street.

Smoking ruins and devastation in the narrow street of St. Stephen's Street looking towards Orford Place.

Man-handling water pumps and hoses, men of the NFS in Rampant Horse Street on the morning of 30 April continue to fight fires after their vain attempt the night before to save some of most famous stores. They were hampered by the low water pressure in the two mains which rendered many hoses useless.

The Clover Leaf
Milk Bar on the
corner of Lower
Goat Lane and
St. Giles Street.

The Norwich Diocesan Teacher Training College on College Road was hit on the night of 27/28 April 1942 and despite the gallant attempts by young students, fires raged in the main hall and chapel.

Ruins of the Norwich Diocesan Teacher Training College.

Ruins of the old Swan Laundry
after a raid in April 1942.

St. Anne's Church on Colman Road.

Devastation to Dereham Road and St. Benedict's (right).

Alexandra Road after the raid on 28/29 April 1942. Julia Agnes Neve, an 85-year old widow, was unable to make it down the steps of the Ferguson family home at 29 Alexandra Road to the shelter and was killed when the house was destroyed. Ernest Burton (56), a bricklayer who ironically worked for the council building air raid shelters, his wife Clara (54) and their children, Sybil (13) and John (19) also died when 46 Alexandra Road was flattened.

Lothian Street.

The first house in the block of church houses known as Jellicoe Terrace in Dereham Road.

Douro Street off Dereham Road.

House on Dereham Road with the staircase intact.

Second of the two houses on Dereham Road that Edward LeGrice photographed.

British Gas Light Company on a corner of Dereham Road.

The Baptist Church on Dereham Road which was badly damaged in the April 1942 bombing.

End of Dereham Road.

Helena Road. On 27 April 1942 at No.8 63-year old Mr. Clare Betts, a brush maker and his 63-year old wife Nellie were killed. So too 68-year old Alice Kate Smith at No.23. At No.10 all three members of the Wallace family died. At No.32 67-year old printer's manager Ernest Albert Hunt and his 70-year old wife Edith died. Agnes Elizabeth Waters (54) and her three children aged 15, 17 and 19 at No.78 were killed when the Anderson shelter they were sheltering at No.76 took a direct hit. The Anderson had been offered to them as their next door neighbours had gone to stay with relatives.

No.1 Merton Road where a bomb exploded in the front garden while the occupants and friends were sheltering in the cellar.

All that was left of the Reverend Robins' house on Dereham Road. Luckily he and his family were away in London at the time of the raid.

The devastated area around St. Benedict's Gate.

Junction of Barn Road and Grapes Hill.

A special constable, his bicycle leaning nearby, directs traffic past the scene of devastation at St. Benedict's Gates after the raid on 29/30 April 1942. The wrecked Midland & Great Northern Joint Railway's rail terminus on Barn Road, which was devastated on the first night of the *Baedeker* Blitz on 27/28 April 1942.

A roof-top view of the damage on the morning after the first raid, looking across St. Benedict's towards the ruins of Morgan's Brewery. The River Wensum can be seen (top centre).

The 'Crown' at 71 St. Benedict's Street, which was damaged in the April 1942 bombing, which wrecked the area.

A roof-top view of the damage on the morning after the first raid, looking across St. Benedict's.

The round tower of St. Benedict's Church was all that remained of the historic church.

The wrecked interior of St. Benedict's Church.

Wrecked houses in a corner of St. Benedict's Alley.

Teams of workmen working at the bomb-cratered St. Benedict's Gate, looking towards the city centre from the foot of Grapes Hill. Many shops and businesses and the last vestige of St. Benet's Gates were destroyed but parts of the city wall survived, as a bomb thought to be not less than 1000 kg struck one of the city's busiest cross-roads.

St. Benedict's Gate
after the raids of
27 and 29 April 1942.

St. Paul's in St. Paul's Square which was gutted by fire on 27 June 1942.

Effect of fire flaking the pillars in St. Bartholomew's Church.

In Heigham Street during the April 1942 bombing, St. Bartholomew's Church had its interior gutted and its bells, fallen from the tower lay half-covered by rubble alongside what remained of the font.

Surface air raid shelters on Aylsham Road.

Wrecked houses on Aylsham Road.

Junction Road.

St. Augustine's Council Schools on the corner of Waterloo Road which were hit by a 500kg bomb.

Waterloo Road.

This UXB buried itself 35 feet deep in Waterloo Park and was removed a month later.

Bomb damage in Patteson Road between Aylsham Road and Waterloo Road. On 27/28 April 1942 all four members of the Jarvis family at No.41 were killed. At No.43 46-year old Army pensioner Walter Goreham died. At No.45 52-year old Sarah Monaghan and her 45-year old brother Patrick Holland and their 78-year old widowed mother Anne Holland were killed. At No.54 Hilda Newby (45) and her 8-year old daughter Barbara died when their house took a direct hit. At No.39 36-year old Laura May Dixon and her 4-year old daughter Isobel were killed and 21-year old Joan Miriam Goddard, an electrical engineering machinist whose husband was serving in the RAF, was badly injured and died in hospital.

The St. Clement's Hill area was badly affected by the April bombing. In Rosebery Road fifty houses were damaged and four houses in Dakin Road were destroyed when a bomb left a huge crater (pictured). Among the casualties in Dakin Road was 16-year old Florence Savory who died at No.26.

Old house in Calvert Street shattered beyond repair had to be demolished.

Terraced houses destroyed on Oxford Street.

Workmen carrying out vital repairs in Caernarvon Road after the bombing.

A cistern blown from the ground floor at Woodlands Hospital onto the roof of the female infirm block.

Woodlands Hospital/The Lodge on Bowthorpe Road (now the West Norwich) was hit on 27/28 April 1942 when Charles Montague Doe, a 63-year old retired ship's fireman and 82-year old Harry Goode, a retired horse trainer, Morris Bowers, an 84-year old retired compositor, Joseph Eagleton, an 81-year old former general labourer, 65-year old Charles Percy Emms, a retired oil vendor, 83-year old William Robert Franklin a former bricklayer's labourer and Charles Aldous a 74-year old former bricklayer's labourer, Jeremiah Lincoln, a 63-year old retired Morgan's Brewery labourer, were killed. Ephraim Austin an 84-year old retired shoemaker died of shock on 7 May as a result of the bombing. When, on the night of 8/9 May bombs were released, apparently at random, in the country districts, mainly to the south east of Norwich, one large bomb added to the already serious damage to the Hospital. The partial demolition of Woodlands Infirmary resulted in the difficult transfer of aged and infirm and deprived Norwich of over 600 non-casualty beds.

Norwich Thorpe Goods Station.

M&GN Railway City Station.

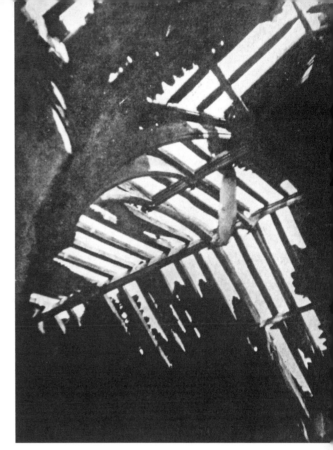

St. Mary's Baptist Chapel and St. Mary at Coslany, one of the oldest churches in Norwich, on St. Mary's Plain, which were gutted on 29 April 1942.

Young boys on cycles pause to glance at the gutted shell of St. Thomas's Church on Earlham Road after the bombing on 28/29 April 1942.

A pall of smoke over Norwich on the morning of 30 April 1942 photographed by F/L P. N. Atkinson flying a Lysander IIIA at RAF Coltishall.

EASTERN EVENING NEWS, Apl. 30, 1942

Black-out—
9.49 p.m. to 5.55 a.m.

WIRELESS—Page 3, Col. 3.

Eastern Evening News

FINAL

No. 18,506—Three 'Halfpence

Thursday, April 30, 1942

SECOND 'REPRISAL' RAID ON NORWICH

Much damage to shopping centre

A.A. GUNS PUT UP HEAVY BARRAGE

ANTI-AIRCRAFT GUNS PUT UP A HEAVY BARRAGE WHEN NAZI RAIDERS MADE THEIR SECOND "REPRISAL" ATTACK ON NORWICH LAST NIGHT.

Though the raid was on a smaller scale than that on Monday night, considerable damage was done, particularly to a large shopping centre.

It is feared that there were numerous casualties, including some killed in public shelters.

Several of the raiders were badly damaged, but their destruction is not yet confirmed. Night fighters finally drove them off.

Civil defence services from outside were rushed to help the local A.R.P., and the firemen successfully concentrated in preventing the spread of flames in the direction of a hospital.

A large block of shops was gutted by fire after direct hits with heavy high explosive bombs.

RAID AS DIVED

Damage to old and new Norwich

ONE of the oldest churches in the city—Early, English— has only its round tower standing, and one of the newest churches, built a few years ago, was destroyed by fire in last night's raid.

One of the oldest public-houses in the city and a modern milk bar are among the buildings which have disappeared.

Low level raid on aero works

Independents win two by-elections

RUGBY AND WALLASEY RESULTS

THE Government has lost two seats to Independent candidates in the Rugby and Wallasey by-elections.

At Wallasey, Mr. George L. Reakes (Independent) obtained a majority of 6012 over the National Government candidate, Alderman John Pennington, chairman of the local Conservative Association.

A second Independent candidate was Major L. H. Cripps, shipowner brother of Sir Stafford Cripps, polled only 1597 votes and lost his deposit.

Then, about an hour later at Rugby, a close fight ended in a victory by Mr. W. J. Browne, Independent, with a majority of only 679, over Colonel Sir Claude Holbrook, the Government nominee, and chairman of the local Conservative Association for 15 years.

Inde...   ...tes hav

The the General Election the figures were: Lt.-Col. J. T. C. Moore-Brabazon (C.) 27,949, Mr. J. Airey (Lab.) 13,491; majority 14,458.

Mr. Reakes, who is a journalist, was a member of the Labour Party until a difference of opinion over Munich. He was Labour's nominee when elected Mayor for Coronation year.

Wallasey became a separate division in 1918, and since then, until to-day, has always returned Conservative with a substantial majority.

Mr. Reakes said after the result to-day: "It is a victory for Churchill, and our enemies will now know that Wallasey wants a vigorous prosecution of the war with a fight to the finish."

RUGBY REVERSAL

The by-election at Rugby was caused by the elevation to the peerage of Capt. David Margesson.

At the general election the figures

EEN 30 April 1942.

The south side of St. Julian's Church from the west end taken perhaps the week of 27 June 1942. The Oberammergau carved reredos survived intact and also the Tabernacle with the Blessed Sacrament inside and remain to this day. The Church was re-dedicated on 8 May 1953.

Carrow Works.

The Blue Mill (Block 70) at Colman's Carrow Works after the raid of 24 June 1942.

On 27 June 1942 the Hebrew Synagogue in Synagogue Street, which took its name from the building, built in 1848, was destroyed. The street no longer exists.

Clearing up in the Grove Road area after Raid 36 on Saturday 27 June 1942.

The shell of the 'Trafford Arms' in Grove Road.

The 'Trafford Arms' after the fire raid of 27 June 1942.

Trafford Road looking towards Eleanor Road.

Incendiary devices which destroyed Caley-Morgan's mineral water factory in June 1942.

All Saint's Green looking along Ber Street.

The remains of R. H. Bond & Sons' department store (now John Lewis) on All Saint's Green destroyed in the bombing on 27 June 1942.

After Bonds' was destroyed
disused buses were used to sell
goods to Norwich housewives.

North aisle of St. Michael at Thorn on Thorn Lane off Ber Street.

Here stood the pre-Conquest church of
St Michael at Thorn.
Destroyed by enemy action
27th June 1942.

Blue plaque on in memory of St. Michael at Thorn on Thorn Lane.

Many fine and historic Norwich churches were reduced to ruins or badly damaged in the *Blitz* but apart from slight damage both the cathedral and St. Peter Mancroft survived. On Saturday 27 June 1942 the cathedral itself was hit by bombs for the first and only occasion when a shower of 61 incendiaries landed on the roof and 36 more fell in an unopened container which hit the transept near the tower. Eight fires broke out on the roof but these were successfully doused before they could do much damage by a party of three men who clambered on to the roof and hauled up a fire-hose.

Damage to the North Transept of the Cathedral after the fire raid on 27 June 1942.

Damage to 66 Cathedral Close after the fire raid on 27 June 1942.

The view from the Castle Mound on the morning of Sunday 28 June 1942.

Tins of baked beans being salvaged from warehouses on Riverside on the morning after the raid on Saturday 27 June 1942 which would be remembered as the heaviest firebomb raid on any town or city in East Anglia during the war. Some 2,500 homes were damaged and two factories and a railway goods yard hit by bombs and incendiaries which caused 663 separate fires. Sixteen people lost their lives and 70 were injured.

Frazer's Joinery at St. Martin's Palace Plain by Whitefriar's Bridge, which was hit in Raid 36 on the morning of Saturday 5 September 1942. The machine-shop suffered a direct hit which demolished the boiler house killing four employees and injured three others. Stephen Toole (39) a fireman in the NFS also died. He left a widow, Elizabeth.

After the *blitz* life went on as normally as possible. Here shoppers pass Purdy's restaurant on Guildhall Hill. There was no large devastated area but throughout Norwich as a whole considerable damage was caused. All sections of life were affected and factories, railway stations, shops, schools, hospitals and churches sustained damage and many buildings were totally ruined. By June 1942 there were 2,000 building operatives at work (about a fifth of whom were Corporation employees, while others came from London – affectionately known as the 'Cockney Sparrows' – and Birkenhead). The demolition of the Corporation Depot did nothing to help first-aid repairs. The gutting of the M&GN Joint Railway Station (Midland & Great Northern; known as the 'Muddle & Go Nowhere') and at Thorpe the LNER (London & North-East Railway) Goods Department were also factors that had to be overcome.

On Tuesday 13 October 1942 HM King George VI paid a surprise visit to Norwich and toured some of the worst-affected areas and was introduced to all manner of personnel from St. John Ambulance and Civil Defence Workers to Home Guard, Nurses, Salvation Army workers, National Fire Service, Police and members of the WVS who paraded outside the City Hall. Among them was Police Inspector Edwin Buttle who had also been awarded the BEM for his work as Bomb Reconnaissance Officer and 15-year-old messenger boy John Grix (pictured, smiling) who lied about his age to be accepted as a CD messenger. He received a British Empire Medal and an illuminated address from Australian Civil Defence workers for his bravery in carrying messages during the April bombing despite suffering acid burns and being blown off of his cycle on five occasions. Despite suffering acid burns he worked throughout a night of heavy bombing. 'It wasn't a case of being brave,' he said later; 'I just wanted to be involved and to be honest I didn't know what I was letting myself in for.' John Grix went on to work for forty years at Laurence & Scott. He always regarded his brief encounter with fame as a 'nine-day wonder'.

Accompanied by town clerk and ARP Controller Bernard Storey the King took time to talk to people like Mrs. Ruth Harvey the MAGNA (Mutual Aid Good Neighbours' Association) organiser (centre). The King told Mrs Hardy 'There is too little friendship in the world today. Do keep up the wonderful work when the war is over.'

HRH The Duke of Kent at a bombed out site in Norwich.

Harmer's clothing factory in St. Andrew's Street, which was destroyed on Monday 18 March 1943.

Memorial plaque at the Garden of remembrance, Earlham Cemetery. (Author)

Aerial view of Norwich with Earlham Cemetery in the foreground. (Author)

Albert George Smith (50) a shoe operator (clicker) and ARP warden, who was injured at 56 Alexandra Road, Norwich on 29 April 1942 and died next day at The Lodge (Woodlands Hospital) on Bowthorpe Road. His wife Kathleen Minerva Smith died suddenly on 18 February 1945 aged 53. (Author)

Bibliography and Further Reading

An Artist's War: A Unique Portfolio of Norwich in the Second World War by Philippa Miller (January 2005)

EDP Norfolk Century 1999 edited and designed by Trevor Heaton

Norwich In The Blitz: An Evening News Special Edition

Norwich: The Ordeal of 1942 by E. C. LaGrice

Assault Upon Norwich: The Official Account of the Air Raids On The City by R. H. Mottram

Norwich – A Shattered City: The Story of Hitler's Blitz on Norwich and Its People, 1942, by Steve Snelling (Halsgrove, 2012)

Norwich at War by Joan Banger (Albion Books 1974, 1982)

Norwich Under Fire: A Camera Record: 'The Blitz: City's Week of Terror' (articles in the EDP marking the 55th anniversary) April 1997.

The Story of the 1942 German Baedeker Raids Against East Anglia by Bob Collis published by N. & S. A. M.

Evening News Images of Norwich (Breedon Books, Derby 1994)

Norfolk In The Second World War: A Pictorial History 1939-1945 by Neil R. Storey (Halsgrove 2010)